Cover photo: The sky, sea and shore n

This is a not-for-profit book. After ⌣⌣ ⌣ ⌣
money we receive will go to WaterAid. This will be a minimum
of £4 for every book sold.

Clean water is essential for life, but one in eight of the world's
population does not have access to it. This, and lack of safe
sanitation, result in over two million people dying from water-
related diseases every year. The lack of clean water close to
people's homes also affects people's time, livelihoods and
quality of life.

WaterAid and its partners use practical solutions to provide safe
water, effective sanitation and hygiene education to the world's
poorest people. They also seek to influence policy at national
and international levels.

If you wish to find out more about WaterAid and perhaps make
a further donation to their life-giving work, please see:
www.wateraid.org.uk if you are in the United Kingdom, or
www.wateraid.org if you are elsewhere; or you can write to:
Supporter Services, WaterAid, 47-49 Durham Street,
London SE11 5JD

Thank you for helping us provide sanitation and clean water for
some of the poorest people on earth.

Richard and Celia Walker

You may be able to tell that some maps in this book are drawn
freehand. Any accuracy is purely fortuitous!

On pages 214 and 215 there is an Ordnance Survey Opendata map to
show three voyages. You will need a magnifying glass to study it.

WALKERS
— *in the* —
LIGHT

Richard and Celia Walker

Published by Richard and Celia Walker
ISBN: 978-0-9568015-0-0
Copyright © 2011 Richard and Celia Walker

ACKNOWLEDGEMENTS

We would like to thank all those who have helped us in many different ways: those in the church who have been our fellow pilgrims and from whom we have learnt so much; those who supported and advised us in these and other projects; those in our family and among our friends who have put up with our vagaries, and frequently given us hospitality in their homes. They are too numerous to name but we are grateful to them all.

Richard and Celia Walker

Contents

Walkers in the Light

1 John 1

5   This is the message we have heard from him and declare to you: God is light; in him there is no darkness at all.

6   If we claim to have fellowship with him yet walk in the darkness, we lie and do not live by the truth.

7   But if we walk in the light, as he is in the light, we have fellowship with one another, and the blood of Jesus, his Son, purifies us from all sin.

8   If we claim to be without sin, we deceive ourselves and the truth is not in us.

9   If we confess our sins, he is faithful and just and will forgive us our sins and purify us from all unrighteousness.

This excerpt from the first letter of John in the Bible is expressing a conundrum:

God is sinless.
We cannot be in him if we are sinful.
We are sinful.
We hope to be in him.

It is solved by verses 7 and 9 which say that because of Jesus' sacrifice on the cross, if we come to Jesus, confessing our sins and throwing ourselves on his mercy, the effects of our sin will be removed.

The title *Walkers in the Light* is not intended to claim any virtue for us. We hope the cover photo gives clues as to what the title means. The sun is definitely present. It is shining on the earth which is in darkness. There is blue sky visible.

The problem of our evil is a huge problem in theology. We hope one day to be in heaven with God. But there is no evil in God. We can only be in God if we are without evil. But we are and do evil – in our selfishness, our uncaring, our lack of respect for truth, our unwillingness to let God be our guide, and in so many other ways.

The Bible does not see sin as the occasional misdemeanour of an individual in an otherwise blameless life. We are not all good except for the little naughty things we may sometimes do. Still less does it see sinners as just the monstrously evil people who we read about in the newspapers or the history books: the mass murderers, rapists or child molesters. It describes sin as the normal activity of all humans, who through not caring, or deliberate selfishness, place themselves in opposition to God.

This is the ordinary people – including well-to-do folk, working hard, earning and spending and saving their money, devoted to their families. Many of these people see themselves as *good*. If tragedy befalls them, the press will call them *innocent*. It is us. But measured against God's standard we find ourselves falling short. If we examine ourselves through God's perfect eyes we find ourselves committed first of all to our own comfort, and caring very little for the welfare of others.

God offers us life – not just living and breathing but a new quality of life. There are two words: *Everlasting* and *Eternal*. Everlasting just means forever. But eternal implies not only forever but of a perfect quality. God offers us not just everlasting life but eternal life. This is a life with him as constant companion and friend; one who accepts us and loves us without a hidden agenda or manipulation; one who is prepared to speak the truth to us; who really knows us as we are, and yet keeps loving us. Eternal life is not just after death. It begins now, and gives our life today a new quality and joy.

Jesus said, "I have come that you may have life, and have it to the full." John 10:10

God offers us this, and yet we do not trust him. We give only our small change. We think mainly of our own and our family's convenience. We manipulate the truth to our own advantage. We blame God when things go wrong yet we make little attempt to please him when they go right.

We inhabit a dim world and we are up to our necks in its darkness. God calls us to live in his light – to try to please him and to accept his forgiveness when we fail.

The Bible says that only Jesus' death on the cross takes away the consequences of our sin and puts us in good relationship with God. In his death Jesus *became sin* as Paul writes in 2 Corinthians 5:21. This expresses how he was cruelly separated from his Father; the eternal life that Jesus shared with his Father was taken from him – a much more painful thing for him than even the terrible physical act of crucifixion.

We can all think of people who have shown great caring and we rejoice in this. But if we talk to them they will usually tell us that this is only a small part of their lives. They too are sinners. However good we are, the main thrust of our lives is dedicated to self. The miracle is that in spite of our lack of commitment to God, his loving-care for us is unfailing.

This book tells something of the story of our Christian journey with some adventures along the way. We are sinful but we know God's love for us. We don't always do what he wishes but we receive his forgiveness and so can be in relationship with him. And we can have fun.

We believe that God has put us in a world which is both dangerous and exciting, which can be explored physically and with our minds. We believe that he wants us to explore it, to develop our skills and experience, as well as to look after it and care about others who also live in it, people and other creatures.

We hope you will enjoy the accounts of some of our adventures and our thinking, and that you too will enjoy walking in the light of God's loving-care of you.

Jesus

Richard wrote: "I can look back and say I was brought up in a Christian family. But my father deserted my mother when I was 4, probably a casualty of the war; and so I had little memory of him. My mother brought up my elder sister, younger brother and me to the best of her ability, and that included the Methodist Church and a Plymouth Brethren Sunday School. She was supported practically by some neighbours, some of her brothers and sisters and my father's parents. Her brother Norman was one I remember eager to encourage me in the faith. I felt that Jesus was my Father.

The big decision my mother made for me was to send me to a boarding school. It was probably influenced by my being a fairly difficult child, but I am sure she thought it would be the best for me. The school offered a bursary which made the fees possible. The fact that it was a school founded for the sons of Christian ministers was pleasing to my mother.

In September 1955 I was taken to the school and left in the care of the preparatory department. No exeats (home leave for a weekend) or visits were allowed in the first term. We had to write home each week and they had to be happy letters because the mail was scrutinised by members of staff before posting. But I was far from happy. The grounds were interesting and exciting, though we were quite restricted in how much we were allowed to explore. I thrived in the academic teaching, though the rules and punishments, and the regimented day were not at all to my taste. We had few choices or opportunities to show initiative. The unofficial power of the younger boys who had been boarders since they were eight years old was frightening. The authorised power of some of the boys only a year ahead of us was wicked. Many of the staff were committed to us and to their subject – but one was a predatory paedophile and I was scared stiff of him.

The school did not allow swimwear in the pool. We swam naked. Somehow this man often seemed to be supervising swimming. We were obliged to be members of the scouts with him as scoutmaster. On the compulsory camps we again swam and ran about naked, and he was always present with his camera. And he took carefully selected boys alone into his room. He forced them to strip naked. Then sometimes he caned them, sometimes he spanked them, and sometimes he caressed them.

When I returned home for the Christmas holiday I told my mother what was going on but she did not seem to understand. Presumably she didn't know what to do about it. And so I was sent back again in January in tears. These things were going on at the same time as we were attending morning and evening services on Sundays to encourage our Christian faith. My faith evaporated.

One of the members of staff with whom I felt comfortable was the physics teacher. In the second summer holiday in 1957 he took me, and two other boys who had no father, on holiday to Salcombe in Devon and then Falmouth in Cornwall. It was here that I learned dinghy sailing. They were wonderful, happy, innocent days and I loved them.

As we progressed through the school we left the paedophile in the Preparatory Department. But I was never happy or comfortable. The academic side was reasonably OK. I was never especially good at sport – and sport was highly valued. Each term a professional hockey, rugby or cricket coach was engaged. He trained those who were the best, for the school teams. The rest of us were given a ball and sent on to rougher ground to get on as best we could with teachers who were not sport specialists.

The times I was really happy was when a friend and I stole out of the dormitory and went to watch badgers in the woods; when we tried to photograph sand martins on the nest by making special nest boxes for them; the times when we walked free on the North Downs.

That there was no God I was certain. Science would explain everything eventually.

In the Sixth form I chose science A levels and mathematics. But I also became interested in modern literature and poetry. I founded a remarkably successful society called SSCEMA. (Science Sixth

Club for Encouraging Music and the Arts) It was a scheme to enable us to go on official trips to London and other places as the Arts sixth-formers did. We went to the theatre and to concerts. We also had a one-act play-writing and acting competition.

My play was about a murderer who had been found guilty and sentenced to death and who was being transported by road to his place of execution. The vehicle was in a road accident with a cyclist, and the prisoner was left alone with the badly injured cyclist. He had to make the decision: to escape and possibly save his own life, or to call the emergency services and give himself up for execution. In a static drama the two sides of his mind tried to persuade him which to do. He sums up:

"I fly a burning plane, and there is one parachute for two people"

Eventually he comes to the decision to go for help, not because of any higher moral authority, but because it is good. But as he leaves the stage to fetch help the cyclist dies!

I chose to read Physics and English at the University of Keele in Staffordshire. I enjoyed the Foundation Year where we studied a wide range of subjects "from Plato to NATO," as they said. I found the freedom, and the fact that girls were present, emotionally disturbing. One of the activities I enjoyed was the occasional evening at the home of the Professor of Physics where topics of relevance to Christians and atheists were debated. It was very crowded with nearly everyone sitting on the floor of the large lounge. Although the debating reached deeper levels than I could grasp I had no doubt that I was on the side of the atheists.

In the second year I found the total non-relationship between the Physics and English a problem. I found both of them difficult and I didn't feel that there was much sympathy from the staff for my problems. They probably thought me an odd-ball. I became quite lonely. And then on 5th December 1963 something happened.

It was the end of the day and I was having a bath. Suddenly it seemed to me that Jesus was with me. I saw nothing and heard no voice, but he was there. It was a moment of affirmation.

Something like: "You used to be my friend. I'm still yours." I knew immediately that my life would never be the same again. As I went to sleep I made one decision: not to tell anyone!

The following morning I got up and set off for breakfast in the refectory. It was the custom for people coming out of their rooms at the same time to walk across together. My neighbour, Peter, came out at the same moment as me. We walked across together. I don't think we said anything. If we did it certainly didn't relate to Jesus Christ or the experience I had had the previous night. But Peter said, "You've changed, what has happened?" I assured him that I hadn't. But he was not convinced and pressed me. Eventually I told him of my experience. His reply astonished me. "I'm not surprised," he said, "we've been praying for you."

In a few days he sent me off to see Professor Donald Mackay, of the Communications Department. *The Prof.* invited me for a walk in the country and as we wandered he answered my questions. He was very much more intelligent than me and so I rarely understood what he was saying. But I felt it a great privilege that he was prepared to give time for me. He told me that every Christian should be a member of a church. Although he was a Scottish Presbyterian he told me, "There should be room for you in the Church of England."

He sent me to see the Anglican Chaplain who told me that I must know everything about the Christian faith (He was very wrong) and that what I needed was to be confirmed. Within a few weeks, with no preparation by him, he took me to Lichfield where I confirmed my baptismal vows in the presence of Bishop Stretton Reeve of Lichfield. To be frank the confirmation meant nothing to me but from those days to this, though I had much to learn, and much to experience of God's love, I have never doubted that Jesus is my constant companion and friend.

A funny thing happened a few months later. The same Anglican Chaplain had the bright idea that all the Anglicans should lead services in local churches one Sunday evening. I had become friends with Celia by now and we were sent out on this January evening to St Michael's Church, Stone. We contacted the rector by phone and he promised us some supper after the service – an attractive proposition as the university refectory didn't serve meals on a Sunday evening. The coach that took us was late and we can remember the Rector silhouetted in the church doorway wondering where these students were.

Even though Celia had been a Christian all her life and I was very young in the faith, it was I who was delegated to preach. Celia led the prayers. All the services had the same theme: "The kingship of Christ". I said that for many people Jesus had become a constitutional monarch with no real authority in our lives. After the service we were invited back to the rectory. We talked with the rector and his wife. I wondered where the supper was as I was getting hungry! The rector said he was sure that I would be ordained. I assured him this was not in my plans. I was preparing to be a teacher. Surprisingly he made me promise that when I was ordained I would write to him. It was an easy promise to make as I had no doubt at all that I would never be ordained.

Eventually (at about 9 o'clock) the rector announced that it was time for supper. His wife brought it from the kitchen: cocoa and biscuits!

20 years later, after a long time of not thinking about ordination, God showed me that his ways are not always my ways. He called me into the ordained ministry of the Church of England. It was quite sudden, in the evening of 5th April 1983, and totally unexpected by me. Again it was an almost physical feeling – an awareness. There was no sound and no vision. But the feeling was quite definite. It was almost as if God had said to me, "You are ordained."

Embarrassingly, my first response was to be angry. My impression of Anglican clergy was not one of admiration. My impression of the church, based mainly on the small church of which we were members, was that it was full of elderly people who ran bazaars and summer fetes and rarely did anything demonstrably Christian. These impressions may not have been either kind or wholly accurate. Nonetheless they were my impressions at the time. I also loved teaching physics. I enjoyed the young people and thought that being a vicar would take me away from youngsters. When I became a clergyman I found in Guildford and even more in Bradley the church was full of young people. Indeed for much of the second half of the time we were in Bradley half the church congregation was under 40 years old.

I kept my promise. Before I was ordained in Guildford Cathedral on 29 June 1986, I wrote to the now-retired Rector of St Michael's Church, Stone and invited him and his wife to the service. He was now quite elderly and felt that Guildford was too far from Stone (where he still lived). But they did attend my induction in St Martin's Church Centre, Bradley, 4 years later. When he replied to my first letter he said he did remember the occasion of our visit – "and didn't we have supper in the rectory afterwards?"

Anger

I was an angry teenager. I was angry with my family for deserting me in the boarding school and separating me from friends. I was angry with the school for its hypocrisy and its elitism. The paedophile was left behind in the Preparatory Department (the first two years for me) but his role was taken over to some extent by prefects in my 3rd and 4th years. They slept in our dormitory. When the prefects came to bed they often woke us up and then sometimes practised hitting the wall with a gym shoe before calling out an arbitrary name or two for beating. It seemed an almost weekly ritual – unsupervised by the staff. I held the place in contempt.

The only joys I had were in spite of the school. My friend Roger Durman was interested in natural history. He used to fill in record cards of the birds nesting in the grounds. He and I used to steal out of the dormitory late at night and watch badgers near their sett. I helped him make wooden nest boxes for sand martins which we had observed in a local quarry. They were quite intricate. We made boxes out of wood, each with a plywood tunnel at the front. The back wall of each box was made of two sliding panels, one of glass and the other of wood. The idea was to take photographs from behind a wall of sand that had been left on top of the quarry. We bored holes with cutlery we had borrowed from the dining hall and put the nest boxes in place on two very cold afternoons in January. But when we returned from the Easter vacation bulldozers had demolished the cliff and the boxes were gone.

A poem I wrote at the time:-

> This hollow world of yellow sand,
> where aerie spirits live,
> unworried by a mundane purse;
> a changing, constant universe,
> built and destroyed by man's unknowing hand.
>
> What sadness have you that are free?
> Warm sand breeds no remorse.
> Can scissor-flit on tenuous wings;
> can live, can love can ….. lose all things.
> How can they know who look but do not see?
>
> Dull fleck beneath the dappled dome,
> sleek nomad, twist and dive.
> Fly in demented happiness;
> your world a dusty wilderness
> for they just sign and smash your bill-pecked home.

Another friend Frank Webb and I used to go out at night and walk by moonlight through the lanes. We both hated school and enjoyed being away from it. Once we left a window ajar in the science block. In the night we broke in and climbed up through a trapdoor on to the flat roof. We then ran a long rubber tube up to a Bunsen burner and cooked sausages sitting on the roof. We had not realised until we were clearing up after our midnight meal that the staff accommodation was higher than the science block roof. If a member of staff had looked out of their window we would have been seen – but we were never caught in that or other *illegal* activities.

Frank and I made a tent from parachute nylon and hitch-hiked to Glen Coe in Scotland. One day we climbed a mountain with no map, no climbing equipment, no expertise, and telling no-one where we were going. The climb up was easy. We decided to go down the other side which was very steep. There was a chimney with loose scree. When we realised it was dangerous to go on, we found we were unable to go back as the loose stones slipped from under us. At one point I fell and slid down on to a ledge where Frank was. He stopped me falling to what would have been certain death. We sat on the ledge for over half-an-hour in silence - thinking – before continuing. Eventually we climbed right down – but we were lucky to get away with this escapade.

Being at boarding school meant I lost my friends at home. I had invitations to go on holiday abroad with students who lived in Geneva and Morocco but we could not afford it. Every vacation I came home and looked round the house. I was angry because nothing had changed – and angry if I found any change! At school there was obvious preference given to fee-paying students and discrimination by some of the staff against those of us with bursaries, who were not the sons of ministers. I felt neither part of the school nor home.

When I went into the Sixth-form, as well as continuing to be committed to science, I began to read modern poetry and plays. These focussed my sense of frustration and anger.

As I left my teenage years there was nothing organised about my anger. And when I became a Christian at university my anger was not at first diminished. I hated the comfortable lives of people living in a world where others were starving. I felt that Christians should show a much better example. But the churches I knew were full of wealthy people looking only after their own comfort, as I saw it.

I got to know Celia at university. We used to walk miles through the Staffordshire countryside. I don't know how she put up with my railing against injustice and hypocrisy. So many things became symbols of what I despised; for example silly things like dinner services in white china. When we were married we asked for a Wedgwood Pennine service which was brown. Such was my confusion. But Celia's gentleness, patience, loyalty and love for me and for others taught me a great deal.

Letters from Ghana

On her 21st birthday I asked Celia to marry me. We had talked so much about our goals and dreams that the question was just a formality but it was wonderful when she consented. The previous day I had asked her father for his permission. As soon as she was 21 this would not have been necessary but it seemed the right thing to me."

We graduated at Keele on the 29th June 1966, and were married at St Andrew's Church, Hove three days later on 2nd July. Celia made her own wedding dress. Our parents and other members of the family helped us greatly with all the preparations. We enjoyed a week's honeymoon in a tiny cottage in the northern Lake District lent to us by John Norsworthy, a wonderful Christian, my mother's employer, and a great family friend.

A few months previously we had written to Voluntary Service Overseas offering to go anywhere they sent us as teachers. They replied that their policy was that married couples should both be employed as volunteers, that it was consequently difficult to place them, and that therefore they had nothing to offer us. We were very disappointed. Richard wrote back in anger, not expecting to hear from them again. He said that Third World countries often expected people to be married fairly young, that we were both qualified teachers expecting both of us to make a useful contribution, that there must be thousands of schools throughout the world that would be pleased to have us, and if VSO would make the effort they could easily place us. We were amazed to receive offers of interviews almost by return.

We accepted placements at Mawuli Secondary School at Ho, in Ghana. After a briefing course in the Selly Oak Colleges in Birmingham we flew to Accra by Bristol Britannia in September 1966. These are excerpts from Celia's letters to her parents from Ghana.

University of Accra, Legon. 14 Sept.1966

Dear Mum, Dad and Derek,

After the delayed take-off (because of a fault on the radio set), we had a good non-stop journey, with only a few bumps from rough weather, and touched down at 7.45pm (your time). Our route can easily be plotted if you draw a line from Gatwick to Palma and another from Palma through Algiers and Gao to Accra. We flew at about 19,000 ft. at 350 mph, and often the ground was obscured by cloud, but we could see from Newhaven right beyond Shoreham as we said goodbye to England. We then watched the changing field patterns over France, then Spain, with the countryside becoming drier, from greens to yellowish brown. As we passed over Barcelona and met the Mediterranean it really was a beautiful blue. Soon it was Algiers and the Atlas Mountains, yellow and brown again, and then the Sahara, hot orange and red, patterned with dunes, looking from our height like patterns on the seashore, or sometimes mountains and hills of grey, with plains in between covered by fans of outwashed debris.

About six o'clock it was beginning to get dark. I had hoped to see the Niger River but thought it was now too late, for the sky and land had become one in a soft grey. Then we saw a silver line on the horizon, and as we passed over with (luckily) the plane dipped to our side, it was like a great roll of silver cloth on the blue-grey, and beaded with islands. After a short fiery sunset it was quickly dark and in an hour we had landed.

The customs check was amazingly quick; nobody's bag was looked at, but there were long queues to exchange money and for checking entry permits. We all posed for a photo for the *Graphic* and were then whisked off by coach to the University, and a very hard bed, but a good night's sleep.

We are staying at the university until Friday, when we will be taken by State Transport bus to Ho. This morning we had talks from an African Professor on *Ghana Today*, and the Deputy Education Officer on *The Education System*. This afternoon we had a quick coach trip around Accra, saw some of the new buildings, some crowded African quarters, the sea, coconut palms, dishes on heads, babies on backs, bright coloured clothes and children wanting to be photographed. Tomorrow we have talks on teaching techniques and a chance for questions. In the afternoon we are going to the Botanical Gardens, and in the evening to a reception at the Ministry of Education for us, the Peace Corps and Canadian volunteers. Later in the evening we are promised a demonstration of traditional dancing and drumming.

So far I have not been too hot. It has been mostly overcast today with a cool breeze - but not chilly enough to want a blouse with sleeves.

We have been warned that parcels may be heavily charged with duty, especially Christmas presents etc. So please do not send unless we ask.

Our very best love to all. Will write again as soon as possible.

Celia and Richard

Mawuli - 24 Sept. 1966

Thank you for your letter which arrived yesterday. We have now been at Mawuli (the name means *God is*) for eight days, and such a lot has happened that I shall have to spread the telling of it over several letters.

First of all we have beaten you and moved five days after we arrived! We started off in a very pleasant bungalow but it really was too large for us. On Tuesday evening the headmaster arrived and suggested we moved into a smaller bungalow with a stove, fridge, a good work surface and plenty of cupboards in the kitchen. This was left empty because the East German family who had it last year were not allowed an exit permit by the East German government when they wanted to come back from their summer holiday.

The bungalow outside is cream, grey and turquoise, and has a small veranda with a plant like a large convolvulus growing up its supports. Inside there is again turquoise paintwork, with walls of pale green and grey and there are grey lino-tiles on the floors. From the veranda are large doors, which can be folded back, giving a complete open side on a hot day. These open into a lounge/dining room which itself leads on to the kitchen and the backyard. Along a passage leading from the lounge are a study, two bedrooms, bathroom and toilet. The bungalow is furnished with standard issue mahogany furniture which nevertheless is very good and comfortable.

Ghanaians are most friendly people and many have called to bid us welcome. We have had visits from teachers in neighbouring bungalows, students we will soon be teaching, and the school chaplain. The expatriates have also been very friendly and we have been to spend evenings with some of them already. There are two Dutch families, one West German, one British, one Indian and one American. We were met in Ho by the other VSO, Erik, who has entertained us to breakfast and been useful in showing us round.

The evening we arrived we had dinner with the headmaster Mr Banini and his wife. She served wonderful thick, lumpy custard which Richard manfully struggled through. Since then we have had presents of grapefruit from Mr Banini's son who grows them but does not like them, a paw-paw from our houseboy John's brother, some doughnuts from an American and cakes from the West Germans.

Contrary to what we expected this is a boarding school. The students arrived back yesterday, and teaching begins on Monday. There are about 470 boys, 120 girls. Final numbers won't be known until the lower sixth has been shared out among the various Ghanaian schools. Richard is the only physics teacher and until last weekend I was the only English teacher. Fortunately two other English teachers have been found otherwise English would have had to be taught by non-specialists.

[Celia does not mention how nervous and incompetent we were on our arrival. We had nothing to eat because we didn't know where to buy anything and we didn't have the sense to ask. That first weekend a girl VSO, who was going to work in Hohoe further north, was stranded in Ho so we put her up. She told me, when I met her in Oxford nearly 20 years later, that she had stayed in Ho for the weekend with a strange young couple, and we had lived on one tin of sardines! Then we locked ourselves out of our house. John Tsigbe, a youngster of 19, came to our rescue by borrowing a key from the headmaster. He asked if we needed a houseboy. We didn't have the confidence to say, "Yes" but told him we would think about it and he could come round *first thing tomorrow morning*. We found him waiting outside at 5.00 am!]

Mawuli - 2 Oct. 1966

We've done a week's teaching now and are beginning to feel that we are part of the teaching staff. The first few days of term were chaotic and very little teaching was done, but by the end of the week we had got underway. The first big problem was the issue of textbooks. There is a terrible shortage of books and the students have to sign for each one they are allowed.

Richard has had fewer problems with books but there is no graph paper in Ho and he needs this for sixth form work. He also has no darkroom for optical experiments and at the moment he is devising methods of fixing one up. He is very happy to have a lab to himself. His chief problem is Daniel, his lab assistant, who needs constant supervision, and is always likely to be 1½ hours late. He is the headmaster's brother and is often asked to do jobs for him. He has failed O level chemistry and physics and now tells Richard he wants to join the Lower Sixth physics class. Richard doesn't mind him sitting in but feels that he is not up to coping.

The Admin Block of Mawuli School with the Physics Labs behind

I have been encouraged by the standard of spoken English, (I haven't received any written work yet). My upper sixth seems lively and thoughtful. Richard says his upper sixth are very intelligent. It is great fun to have some 6th form teaching and discuss texts with them - though a great responsibility to work them hard enough for exams, and hard work for me as I haven't read several of the texts that they are doing.

As far as domestic matters go things are progressing. John has so far proved very useful and capable. He seems intelligent, works hard and sees many jobs without me having to point them out. He is clean, cheerful, punctual and quick to learn. I do have to be clear with my instructions. Last week I gave him a holdall full of clothes which I asked him to wash. He was very thorough and the holdall too was soon spick and span. His worldly possessions seem to be two shirts, two pairs of shorts, one pair of sandals, a Biro and a book and an occasional newspaper. For his 7 pounds 10 shillings a month he works a six-day week of long hours. If he continues working well we shall give him a rise but we have been warned not to pay him too much because it will upset the general houseboy economy. It takes him about 30 minutes to walk into town for the shopping. We send him three times a week and try to go ourselves on a Saturday.

At the moment (Sunday after lunch), it's 85°F in the shade. In the sun it's much hotter. We are sitting in our lounge and some little boys think it's great fun to walk by and wave to the Yahoo (white man). (that's how it's pronounced but I don't know if the spelling is right). Yesterday it poured all morning. We had to postpone shopping plans till the afternoon. We also had a visit from a VSO and two American missionaries from Hohoe (pronounced hoffway – in fact the correct Ewe is almost unpronounceable to us).

Mawuli - 9 Oct. 1966

At church we had a Harvest Festival last Sunday. In some ways this must be a European export for things are harvested all year round, but the date does roughly coincide with the feast of the New Yam. The service was 20 minutes late starting because it was preceded by a funeral. Then, after a long service and sermon with only a short summary in English, there was a christening of about 16 children. Finally everyone gathered outside the church for an auction of the gifts offered.

Harvest Auction outside the E.P. Church in Ho

It would be fun to see Nick (The Rev E Nichol who married us) holding up a live chicken or some long sticks of sugarcane outside St. Andrews. The hymns are sung in Ewe. We have bought a hymnbook and can read it because it is written in phonetics so we know what it sounds like. If it has the same tune as a hymn we know then we can guess the meaning too.

We are gradually settling into teaching, but of course at the moment there is lots of lesson preparation to do. I have to read a lot of texts. The previous English master seems to have picked a very difficult selection; some I haven't read and others I would never try to do with a fifth form in England. Here I shall somehow have to try to get across the necessary background and atmosphere. I have been enjoying myself this week reading up on Chaucer and I'm learning a lot of 14th century history as I read. I hope I can impart some of the enthusiasm to the students. In my fifth form there are students from 16 to 25, which makes for some difficulties.

We have had visits from two Hausa-men this week. These are traders who work throughout West Africa. The first arrived at our door with his white robe and skullcap characteristic of northern Nigeria, but showing his prosperity in a gold wristwatch. His small boy lifted the huge bundle he was carrying off his head and the Hausa-man sat cross-legged on the floor and set out his display, unwrapping each carving from a rag or much used piece of paper, dusting it and setting it up for us to see. Much of his stuff was modern and not very well carved, but we bought a pair of ebony elephant book stands which we liked (Richard's birthday present from me). Richard did some bargaining and we managed to knock one third off his original price.

The second Hausa-man followed much the same procedure, but his English was a little better and he had a smart leather briefcase to store his cash in. From him we bought a leather cover from Chad we can stuff to make a pouffe. It is natural coloured leather, which he said was camel, thonged with green, red and black, making an attractive pattern. We have now spent everything for the month. (I have kept enough for food and to pay John).

We are now used to waking up early and don't often need the alarm. We get up at 6.00, have a small breakfast, assembly at 7.00. More breakfast at 8.45, lunch 1.30 or 2.00 if Richard is teaching last period. Dinner 6.30 or 7.00pm. We try to prepare lessons in the afternoon, and on free evenings we sometimes have a game of Bezique.

Mawuli – Sunday 16 Oct. 1966

The lower sixth came on Friday and lessons for them start on Monday. This is because after O-level results, which are published late in September, sixth form candidates are equally distributed to schools in Ghana with sixth forms.

Yesterday we had hoped to sleep until seven, but at 6.00 am we were woken by the whole school walking by our window. They had been warned by Mr Banini about making too much noise at meals and between lessons, so when the noise did not decrease, and especially when no one would stop talking when the chaplain (who is not very popular with the students) tried to say grace, he ordered the whole school to weed the grounds as a punishment.

The playing field just beyond our house badly needed cutting. So from 6.00 am to 5.00 pm (with breaks for meals and rest periods), there was a constant chatter and shouting accompanying the swishing of cutlasses which even the girls wield very effectively. A cutlass is one of the items which every student has to bring to school. We could tell which prefect was in charge because he carried a small hand bell on his head. We were also amazed to see the whole school turnout the previous Saturday to do the washing in buckets on the grass outside the dormitories. Both boys and girls are very proficient at this, and soon every washing line, bush, and blade of grass was covered with shirts, shorts, kente cloths and towels.

We paid John on Friday. His eyes increased at least 10 times in brightness at the sight of his first pay packet. Today he appeared with a smart haircut, a fairly popular style, short and thinned out at the back, leaving the front longer standing up like a quiff.

This week I'll tell you a little about the food we're having. Ghanaians do not seem to discriminate between cuts of meat: Everything is six shillings a pound, and everything is stewed. Some of the meat is tough so we have tried cooking it in beer. We have also tried roasting some. Most of our meat comes from the cold store. The State Fishery also has a cold store in town. We can also buy small eggs. At present yams are in season. Soon, we are told, cassava will be the potato substitute. Yams grow in the ground and look like huge carrots (about 10lb each). Their leaves have to be supported on a pole like runner beans. We eat boiled yam in pieces or mashed. It makes excellent chips and is also good for *potato* cakes. When we don't have yam we have boiled rice. I have taught John to make an excellent risotto. We can get cabbage sometimes, but we eat a lot of cocoyam leaves which cook like spinach. John's speciality is stuffed peppers. These, and green beans, we get from a market garden attached to the school. They also have broccoli and carrots which will be ready soon. John makes a good sauce with tomatoes and onions and the Ghanaian version of peanut butter for thickening, with cayenne pepper for flavour. Oranges, grapefruit (which they call grapes), bananas, paw-paws and pineapples are all available. Children often come to the door with a tray of oranges or a large pineapple on their heads.

Things like cooking oil, sugar and butter are usually obtainable from the shops in town. Sometimes they run out so we stock up when we can. So you can see that we won't starve, and John looks after us very well.

Mawuli – Sunday 23 Oct. 1966

Yesterday we went with John to Ho big market. There is a small food market every day, but every four days there is an incomparably larger affair when a great deal of food is brought in from surrounding villages. Also torches, cloth, mats, jewellery, sandals, loofahs etc. are sold. We set out just after eight to walk into the town. Before we got here a British Council representative said that the town was like Bradford. The similarity he was pointing out is that the town is in a basin in the hills. We are on the hill on one side and from our dining room we can see the hills on the other. We can't see the town as it is in the hollow. The Electricity Office is part the way up the hill on the other side of town. We went there first to let them know the date we occupied our house. We caused quite a diversion and clerks rushed around to bring us seats, and they even found a stool for John.

The town looked beautiful from a distance. On our left was the hill scarp, roughly wooded in parts and covered with a rich green. On our right was a plain with isolated hills rising from it. Ahead of us, across the town, was Mawuli Secondary School, hidden by trees. The town itself, white and yellow, a mixture of mud and thatch, concrete and corrugated iron, some parts gleaming in the sun, others sheltered under groves of coconut palms, was below. Close to, the heat, smell and noise, made the town's beauty less obvious.

The market is on the edge of town and covers an area about the size of the Goldstone Ground with three or four sheds, like the North Stand minus terraces. It was covered by a mass of buying and selling as congested, colourful and noisy as a football crowd. [The Goldstone Ground was the home ground of Brighton and Hove Albion Football Club, close to where Celia's parents lived.]

Women traders sat patiently on the ground with what they had to sell spread before them on leaves: a few tomatoes, a paw-

paw, onions, a few cubes of sugar. Chickens with their feet tied lay patiently waiting too. A few vultures with shoulders hunched sat amongst them waiting for what they could steal.

This week I have marked some third form essays on *My Town*. I feel as though I have been given a guided tour of the Volta Region from the lagoons and fishing villages on the coast through some of the more important market towns, cocoa growing areas, small villages depending on subsistence agriculture, and new ones built to house those whose homes are now under the Volta Lake. I feel I have learnt a lot from them. The important status symbols in a town or village are tarred roads and street lighting, and houses made out of cement and concrete and corrugated iron rather than mud and sticks. Community centres, stores and banks get an honourable mention in many cases. Not one student omitted a list of educational institutions if their place had any. They are all very proud of their towns and defend them by mentioning the community spirit, Sunday gatherings for football or tribal drumming, and how people always come back for Christmas and Easter.

Yesterday evening we entertained the other VSO, Erik, and the American, Pearl, who is Head of Science, and taught them Bezique which they seemed to enjoy.

Mawuli – Sunday 29 Oct. 1966

Today we had hoped to go to Accra; we wanted to visit the university bookshop and get one or two things for the house. Just before our alarm (set at 4.15) went off, we woke to hear the sound of talking drums and much singing and shouting carrying from the town, and were puzzled as to what it might mean since we hadn't heard of any festival being held. Shortly after five, while it was still dark, and when we had breakfasted on bread, bananas and coffee, we set off towards the centre of the town. The bus was due to leave at 5.30. Although we couldn't see them in the dark, we could hear people all around us preparing

35

breakfast, or drawing water while the day was still cool. Still there was the sound of the drums, and as we walked further into the town we could hear wailing and crying. We arrived at the bus stop a few minutes before the bus was to leave, and joined the ticket queue. But a few people in front of us, the tickets ran out, and as there are only two buses, and the return journey in a day is impossible on the afternoon bus, we walked sadly home. We will try again next Saturday.

Instead of having a spending spree we are putting in a good day's work, preparing lessons, marking books, writing lesson records, and typing stencils of questions, tests or comprehension passages to use with our classes. Richard has been enjoying himself looking through catalogues of school physics equipment and making out an order for £351.

We began work at 6.15 a.m. John arrived at his Saturday time of 7.30 ready to put in a day in the garden and was surprised to see us. We asked him about the talking drums. He can't interpret them as he says they generally speak in Twi, the

Ashanti language, not Ewe, but he said that a linguist had died yesterday. A linguist is a man appointed to speak on behalf of the chief because the chief never gives his orders direct. We were hearing the wake-keeping. The funeral bell at the EP (Evangelical Presbyterian) Chapel has also been tolling throughout the day.

We have been asked to sponsor the school Student Christian Movement (SCM). We held the first Bible study last week. 46 students turned up and filled our living room. Richard led it very well. As well as Bible studies the SCM here also has debates. Richard was asked to chair one last night on the motion: *Should Christians Divorce?* The speaking varied a great deal in quality, and points were not always logical or helpful to the side which raised them. But everyone seemed to enjoy it. I thought Richard did an excellent job in summing up the miscellany of points and making the issue votable. [The reader is asked to remember that Richard was just 23 years old. In Ghana we were often asked to behave and respond in ways beyond our years and outside our experience.] The debate was held in the largest classroom, the science lecture theatre, but even then not all who wanted to could get in. Many stood outside listening through the windows. You would have been amused to see the hands pushed at all angles through the louvre windows to vote.

Two Ghanaian scouts came bob-a-jobbing for the old and needy today. It was difficult to find them a job as John is very proud of his work and loath to let anyone else do any. I found them a small sweeping job and they seemed pleased with their 25 pesewas. [A cedi was worth about 10 shillings, (50p). A pesewa was one hundredth of a cedi – so in Ghanaian terms we were generous.]

We have been without water for much of this week. At first John had to fetch it from the rain water tanks at the school, but now there is generally tap water for an hour in the morning and again in the evening so we keep our bath and two buckets full. This isn't a lack of rain; just inefficient town machinery. What we get through the pipes has been brought to the school by tanker. The problem is the water is very muddy.

Mawuli – 27 Nov. 1966

This weekend we have been to an American Thanksgiving Day celebration. There was Turkey and blueberry pie. A large number of Peace Corps attended. Some Ghanaian foods had been added and a group of local drummers invited, so it was a very international party and very noisy and crowded. The party was given by an American girl who has been here about three years and who we met at Sogakope, and an English couple at the secondary school at Kpandu. (Kp is like just p but the K is slightly pronounced)

The State Transport bus service to Kpandu has been discontinued, so we set off just before noon with another American from here, Pearl Snitker, to give us plenty of time for the journey by lorry. Kpandu is only 35 miles north but there are some mountains between Ho and Kpandu. To reach the road which crosses the pass you have to go south on the Accra Road for 13 miles and then turn north again. We were very lucky and found a small lorry due to leave in about half an hour.

We sat under the shade in the lorry park and watched children drawing water at one of the town pumps. When the lorry was almost full the driver beckoned us to get in. White ladies are usually privileged and I was asked to sit in front with the driver. The lorry had been standing in the sun and the seat was so hot I was sure my skirt must be scorched. We drove around the lorry park and up and down the town a couple of times, the driver hooting and shouting out, "Kpandu! Kpandu!" to try to attract some more customers. He found two and we set off at high speed with Richard and Pearl rather cramped in the back, having to keep their heads bent because of the low roof. At one stage

The Lorry Park and water pump in Ho

on the journey there were four of us on the front seat! Fortunately it was over quickly and we were at Kpandu by 2.15.

Travelling on a Sunday is more difficult. There may well be no lorry going your way. The driver who took us there promised he would bring us back, picking us up from school at 9 a.m. after he had washed his lorry. Richard and I wanted to be back for our junior Bible study at 1 p.m., and several people wanted to go to Ho or the junction with the Accra Road, so we walked round the lorry park asking the destination of every likely looking lorry. Eventually we found *Ah Sugar* which was going to the junction and we all got aboard. He set off almost at once, without overloading, and we had a short comfortable ride. We could have waited at this junction for several hours but after about 20 minutes along came a Benz bus and a lorry, both of which looked full. The drivers were not to be defeated, So Richard and I ended up in the Benz bus sitting six on seats meant for four. We arrived safely just after 12, in time for our Bible Study.

As you say the water situation is serious but I think the school will only have to close if the pump is not mended before the dry season. Fortunately the dry season isn't long here. As long as the tanker continues to bring water to the school we shall be alright even though it does only flow for one hour a day. John has somehow obtained an empty oil drum for us. He arrived back with it carried triumphantly on his head.

Things may be more serious in the town. When we were in Kpandu we heard that there were several typhoid cases from Ho in the local hospital. When water doesn't flow from the town taps people get it from any puddle or ditch. When they are really short John's family get water from us. We are glad that we had our TAB jab [Typhoid and paratyphoid types A and B]. We also make sure we boil all our drinking water. This week the water situation in school has been eased as 200 students have been sent home to collect outstanding fees. Of course this will not help our teaching.

Yesterday we had our first experience of the harmattan when dry air from the Sahara covers the country. The temperature rises during the daytime but because of the drop in humidity it feels cooler. The students begin to wear pullovers and scarves. It really does cool in the evening and, except that our lips and eyes feel dry, it is refreshing. The mountains are partially hidden by dust and the setting sun is a glowing red ball.

The school field in harmattan

Cocoyam leaves   Cocoa

Today we got up early and walked up the hill on the other side of Ho to take some pictures of cocoa growing. By seven o'clock it was already getting hot. On the way we saw a snake and a scorpion run over on the road. The largest animal that we have seen was a monkey which was swinging about in a tree near the church. There are termite hills, and we often see ants: quite large ones walking about randomly, and very small ones following each other in lines. [Celia protected her parents from the knowledge that we had seen several snakes, some very close: a green mamba dropped from a tree near the Minister holding a baby during an outside baptism service; Richard leapt over one which reared up at him when he was coming down the steps from his laboratory; a spitting cobra came into our back garden for a short time before retreating.]

The sixth form have a selection of Wordsworth's poems to study for A-level, among them *Daffodils*. I would be grateful if you could look among my postcards for a large coloured one of Wordsworth's *Daffodils*; also, if there is one of the Langdale Pikes I could show it to the fifth form as they are mentioned in one of the poems. The sixth form seem to be enjoying *Great Expectations* [1] and *Emma* [2]. [We certainly worried about the England-centric education which we were involved in. The West African Exams Council set the O-level exams and made them slightly more African, but A-level exams were set in England. One question on an A-level physics paper involved the thickness of ice on a pond!]

We have sent your Christmas present. We hope you won't be disappointed with it - it's a yam. [I don't know why Celia didn't tell her parents the story of the yams: One afternoon we were working in our lounge when a highly polished Rolls-Royce car pulled up outside and a uniformed chauffeur presented us with an envelope, on the back of which was the Royal Crest. We were surprised and all the more so because our house did not have a road to it. The card inside informed us that the British

High Commissioner would be visiting us the following day. The next day the car arrived again. The High Commissioner was represented by his wife as he had had other business. The lady was very pleasant but she clearly thought that she was the Queen, and she irritated me. When she told us that she and her husband were going back to the UK and offered to take anything we wanted in the diplomatic bag, we asked if she could take some Christmas presents. We quickly wrapped up two yams and gave them to her for our parents.]

Mawuli – 16 Dec. 1966

Thank you for your Christmas cards. I am going to show the snow scene to my fifth form, not for the snow, but because I think the trees are elm and illustrate this quotation from one of their set poems: *say, do the elm clumps greatly stand, still guardians of that holy land?* [It is hard to believe that the West African Exams Council would set Rupert Brooke's *Grantchester* as a text for African O-level students even in English literature!]

With the temperature over 90° F. it is hard to realise that it is Christmas, although the students have been singing *In the bleak midwinter* for several weeks. We have now finished marking end of term tests and writing reports and today the school broke up for the holiday.

Last weekend we went to a party at Winneba on the coast towards the West. VSOs from all over the country were invited. Winneba beach is lovely – cool breeze, a stretch of shining sand, shells, rocks and rolling breakers. No good for swimming but popular with white people from Accra. The only Africans on the beach were mending their nets. On our way through Accra we bought a Heinz Christmas pudding and a jar of Chivers mincemeat at exorbitant prices.

We had our staff Christmas feast this week. Ghanaian food for first course: chicken and fish with hot peppery sauce, rice and a dish made of maize flour mixed with palm oil. After this came sponge pudding and custard, which pleased the expatriates apart from Richard. The school also had a carol service. How they enjoy *In the bleak midwinter*. It is difficult to keep a straight face when you know they haven't a clue what it is like, and put on woollies when the temperature plunges to 75° F.

Mawuli – Christmas Day 1966

Richard and I have just finished washing-up after Christmas dinner. We ate our meal sitting on the veranda, temperature 88°F. We had chicken (which John killed and plucked for us yesterday – no polythene bag chickens here), with my own stuffing which I'm very proud of: aubergines, tomatoes, onions fried and mashed together with gari (dry fried grated cassava). We also had aubergines, peppers and plantain, bread sauce and gravy. Then we had our expensive tinned Christmas pudding which we had bought in Accra.

Eating Christmas dinner

Last night we went to a nativity play by the women's Bible Class in the EP Church. Ghanaians just love comic characters and here the shepherds were the source of fun. They danced up and down the nave and in their efforts to see them people stood on the benches they normally sit on; small boys stood on windowsills, and there was a general riot of laughing, talking, singing and even small boys with toy guns and sparklers.

We also went to church this morning 9.30 – 11.30. There was a long sermon in Ewe, fortunately followed by the usual English summary, and we were able to join in the carols.

We have our room decorated with Christmas cards and a paw-paw tree with candles. John cut this from the bush yesterday but it won't last long. It is already drooping.

Mawuli – 6 January 1967

We have, in a somewhat leisurely way, resumed work this week. There is a lot we would like to do before term begins. Before Richard has a chance to read this I had better say that he has been working very hard rearranging his labs, making one into a laboratory for 5th and 6th form only, and the other for junior physics and general science.

He has also been drawing up a scheme of work for forms one to five hoping that the junior classes may get some chance to do practical work. He finds many of his fifth form have a very scrappy knowledge. Often lower down the school they have had sixth form teachers i.e. those who have just got A level and are waiting to go on to some further education. These often just read out the textbook to the class, or get them to learn by heart things they don't understand. Two years ago two Russian teachers were here who spoke little English, so that was another year they didn't learn much physics.

We do have some shortages. Richard had to send to Keele for practical books for the 6th form, and I have only eight English course books for 35. Ho does run out of basics from time to time e.g. flour, sugar, butter, rice. At the moment there is no margarine. We now have a reserve of most things. We have been told many times that things are much improved since Nkrumah was overthrown. There are still large stocks of Chinese goods in the shops showing how much Nkrumah was indebted to China. The Ghanaians are very conscious of their liberation. If I ask a member of the third form to give an example of the use of a particular construction he will drag Nkrumah into his sentence if at all possible, and this is gleefully received by the rest of the class.

The headmaster's son, Wola Banini, one of Richard's fifth form students, occasionally drops in for a chat about 5 or 6 p.m. One day he spent over an hour telling us about the old regime. The school did not have a good reputation; the students asked too many questions when they were given ideology lectures; once they refused to march in the youth parade. The next day about half of Ho was forced to demonstrate outside the school. The press and radio report the trials of those accused of corrupt practices and are full of talk of reconstruction.

This week we have planted some tomato seeds, (from a tomato), and fitted out an irrigation scheme so that all our shower water flows round the tomato beds in a series of channels. It is still harmattan, 87° F. approx. and snowing, but not white. This is the time of year for the burning of the land in preparation for sowing. Everywhere there are fragments of charred grass and other vegetation, floating to earth like snowflakes.

Mawuli – 5 Feb. 1967

Greetings from two tired Walkers! We have been running non-stop with the Science Club trip last weekend and the SCM conference during the last three days. We are now looking forward to the 24th, the first anniversary of National Liberation Day.

Yes, the Nkrumah stamps are old stocks being used up. His likeness is also on the currency, although not for long. Soon the new Cedi is being introduced based on the pound and not the 1d (the old British penny) as it is now. We have just been informed that the February salaries will be paid in new Cedis. We shall be well-prepared for Britain's changeover when it comes.

We covered 700 miles on our Science Club trip. We had intended to visit the diamond mine at Akwatia, but because the bus gearbox had to be sent to Accra for repairs we couldn't leave until Thursday morning and so had to speed on to Takoradi. The Pioneer Tobacco Company there was very impressive. It was fully automated producing 140 million cigarettes a month, providing free meals and medical treatment for employees. The very smart and efficient factory guide gave us all a postcard of the factory to send to a friend in Ghana (we sent ours to John). His offering the students free samples of cigarettes impressed us less! We went in the refrigerated warehouse where the tobacco leaves are maintained at 60°F (15°C). It felt very cold, and when we came out the air was stifling!

Unfortunately it was maintenance day at the goldmine at Obuasi so we were not able to see the ore being crushed or sorted. We did see one sample being tested, the main shafts, and a rescue room. A sample of ore was passed around and the students were keen to receive free samples but a tight watch was kept on them!

We also visited a sugar factory in which sugarcane is processed to make granulated sugar. Sadly, domestic sugar is sold in lumps (5 at a time) and so all the sugar produced by this factory had to be exported. The stalks left when the sugar has been removed, a waste product, is called *bagasse*. The students thought this a very funny word.

In Kumasi we visited the Central Hospital and the zoo. We listened to a doctor speaking, almost with tears in his eyes, of the white cliffs of Dover. Then for some reason we were taken to the place where amputated limbs etc. were burnt. The students suggested this was bagasse too! At the zoo there was a lion which had been given by Manchester Zoo! The keeper of the snakes called Richard over and thrust a large python into his hands, expecting to frighten him. The students stepped back quickly but, with commendable aplomb, Richard wrapped the snake around his neck and told them he was not afraid of snakes.

On Thursday evening we found a tarantula sitting on our veranda: a big spider with black furry legs. John told us it was very dangerous and wasn't impressed when we told him that our medical book said that tarantulas are "loathsome spider-like creatures but their bites, though severe, are neither poisonous nor dangerous."

Mawuli 10 April 1967

We now think it would be right for us to stay on for another year. The science sixth form will double in size and Richard will be especially useful. We have also made inquiries about coming home in the summer holiday, but the Ghana Government, quite reasonably, is only willing to pay fares for a two-year contract. A one-year contract would be a special concession and we couldn't expect them to pay our fares. We could save up enough for return fares (£198 each) but the airlines only accept hard currency so we would have to convert our savings into pounds. Ghana has a balance of payments problem even worse than Britain so that would not be helpful to them. We would also prefer to spend any spare money importing books and science equipment, and to send John to school. He had to give up secondary school because he couldn't get the funds. So we think we will not be returning to England in July. [In the end the Ghana Government did pay our fares and we did return to England for 5 weeks]

We enjoyed our Easter trip to Amedzofe which is in the mountain area of the Volta Region. We stayed with the VSOs there in the highest house in Ghana. From their veranda we could see the Volta Lake and further to the mountains in Togo. Because it is so much cooler there we were able to go on several walks including one through the forest to a waterfall. We also had a game of tennis on a very battered court and enjoyed the work of 50 enthusiastic ball boys.

Celia and another VSO walking near Amedzofe

Mawuli 11 June 1967

A Trust Fund has been established to care for the widows and children of those killed in the abortive coup. Yesterday the board of trustees launched the appeal in the Volta Region at a special meeting held at the Regional Headquarters Offices. All the children and teaching staff walked across town to get there. There were speeches, a drumming group and palm branch shelters for protection from the sun during the long proceedings. A band played the theme from Handel's Judas Maccabeus interminably. As the contributions were delivered, the names of the donors and the amounts given were announced over the public address system. We find this a strange custom, but even when there are special collections at church, the whole list of donors with amounts is read out.

Please excuse the writing but as the sun is not too hot we are sitting out in the garden. We can hear the singing at the EP morning service. In fact we are practising sunning ourselves, ready for a trip north in a few weeks time. We hope to take a party of fifth and upper sixth students to Yendi, about 200 miles north of here, to help in building a new chapel, from the 3rd - 14th July.

[Celia probably didn't have time to write to her parents, after the Yendi expedition, before we saw them when we went for the break in England. We took the school bus with driver as we had done on the Science Trip. The whole journey was on red laterite roads. We were welcomed by the local pastor whose wife had prepared a meal for us. Their house had mosquito netting at the door and windows but these were left open and served to trap insects inside rather than keep them out. The meal on a table was covered with white cloths. When these were removed they revealed hundreds of flies, some flying, some swimming in the soup and some drowned in it! We ate the meal (flies and all) but after that delegated two students each day to assist with food preparation and try to solve the problem.

Each morning we assisted a builder with mixing mortar and carrying concrete blocks from a pile where they had been left from the expedition from Mawuli School the previous year. We had to inspect the blocks carefully when we picked them up because small black scorpions were hiding amongst them.

 The people of north Ghana are mainly Muslim. The Christian community are from the south. Their main intention is to go home south again as soon as possible. They had little interest in

building the chapel. Later each day we visited some places of interest such as the airport control tower where there was a hole in the floor where a bulldog clip was lowered on a piece of string so that the meteorologists below could attach the weather forecast. We also visited a modern technical college supplied by the Dutch Government. It had huge lathes and machines to repair the left-hand drive Dutch cars (also supplied). There were rows of modern electric cookers in the catering department. But the whole college was unused and insect infested. There was no electricity supply for many miles!

On the last evening a goat was slaughtered at a feast for us. Richard, as a guest of honour, was given the intestines of the animal to eat! The next day for the hot and bumpy drive home, with no toilets, he developed dysentery. We spent the night at a Mission Station at Bimbila on the way south. Richard was so pleased to get there!]

Preparations are under way for Honours Day (a sort of speech day). Choirs and soloists have been practising songs for weeks. We think it's a pity that they choose English songs instead of some of their own much more lively ones. Teaching staff are expected to wear academic or native dress. Celia will wear our one academic gown and Richard is going to put on our kente cloth. No cleaners are employed by the school so students have been sweeping and cleaning, cutting the grass with their machetes and generally tidying up.

Last night we had Pearl and Mr Abenny to dinner. Mr Abenny was in the 6th form here two years ago and will now teach here for several years before he can get a grant to go to university. He comes from the Eastern Region and is one of the few non-Ewes on the staff. He teaches Twi, the language of the Ashantis, and takes an interest in music. There are no formal music lessons – just hymn practices.

Mawuli 8 Nov. 1967

Weekends are becoming as hectic as the rest of the week. Every Saturday morning Richard is now busy with physics projects. He and John Stouffer [a Canadian volunteer who lives in a house near us] have students making pinhole cameras, electric motors, model planes etc. and doing various sixth form experiments. For the last two Saturdays I have been helping Pearl draw the timetable neatly so we could post a permanent copy on the noticeboard. Two weeks ago Richard led the Sunday evening service and we entertained the preacher, who was an Englishman, to supper. Last Friday the SCM had a talk on the Authority of the Bible. The lecturer was Dr Tolley, an American teacher at the Theological College at Peki about 30 miles from here. As he had to attend a meeting in Ho on Saturday we invited him and his wife to spend the night with us. We had intended to celebrate Guy Fawkes Night by cooking plantain and sausages over a fire, but I was on duty that day and had to attend meals at school, so we had to postpone this.

A Pakistani biology teacher lives in a nearby bungalow with his wife and small daughter. He is quite friendly but usually chooses awkward times to drop in and be sociable. He invited us to tea last Sunday afternoon and his wife provided some food: chiefly vegetables fried in a sort of batter and served with tomato sauce. Neither his wife nor his daughter ate with us.

John Stouffer has just brought your letter which he found in my pigeonhole. We get on well with him and his wife Kathy. As we live next door we can pop in for breaks between marking etc. in a Keele fashion. Last Sunday they talked to our SCM discussion group about life in Canada.

Last Saturday Mr Banini presented us with an unexpected invitation to dinner. The Stouffers were also there and the Heitings, a young American couple. Mrs Banini always puts on an excellent spread, and caters well for the Europeans considering she hasn't been abroad. We had chicken stew with rice, yam cakes and salad, followed by sponge and custard. Richard managed to negotiate the custard and, during the evening, bravely broached the subject of a half-term break. Mr Banini had obviously forgotten about it, although most of his staff were looking somewhat jaded. So we have this Friday and Monday off. We, together with the Stouffers and Pearl, intend to go to Accra on Friday in the school bus, spend one night there, and then return as far as the dam, and spend a restful weekend in the Akosombo Hotel.

Mawuli – 10 Dec. 1967

We were pleased to receive your letter with comments on devaluation, and also glad to hear that the books are on their way. I hope you fed the camel well beforehand!

Last week the chemistry department received a letter from Ghana's Black Star shipping line asking the school to collect a crate of *dangerous chemicals* direct from the *Sakumo Lagoon* when she docked at Tema. Nobody had any idea what chemicals they were – there was no record of dangerous chemicals on order. The next day Richard heard from Griffin and George that the rest of the Mawuli order had been shipped aboard the *Sakumo Lagoon* on 23 November. This was distressing because the ship had arrived but the school had not yet received a Bill of Lading from England (a document which certifies contents of crates so they can be unloaded without opening for Customs inspection – important when dealing with delicate equipment).

So a hurried trip to Tema took place on Thursday. Richard, Pearl and John Stouffer arrived at Tema to find the ship had already sailed, but fortunately our crates had been unloaded. The problem was to find them. Without the bill of lading they did not know what shape, size and number they were looking for. After a day spent searching through warehouses they found two but had to return to Ho leaving them at Tema. Meanwhile about 4 p.m. Mr Diehl arrived at our house with the offending document. The letter had been registered as it also contained insurance policies and the Ho Post Office had delayed two days before informing us of its arrival. You can imagine the anger of the three weary searchers on their return!

We hope to return to Tema on Friday to pick up the equipment, and then go on to Accra for Christmas shopping. From the Bill of Lading we see that the dangerous chemicals are in fact a box about the size of a biscuit tin labelled *harmless chemicals!*

As you say, Christmas always takes you unawares, but we haven't an excuse even though the weather is hot. The senior house father preached on Advent a full four weeks before Advent Sunday, the students have been carolling for a long while, and Father Christmas arrived at Kingsway Stores on 4 December.

Last year we were disappointed with the school Carol Service, so Richard and John Stouffer have volunteered to organise it this year. We are trying to follow the traditional Nine Lessons and Carols including some Ghanaian carols at suitable points. We also hope to hold a party for the SCM sometime this week, together with Pearl and the Stouffers.

The SCM conference at Jasikan last weekend was good. The local SCM at the training college there had things well organised. They even put on a short play for our entertainment on Friday evening. The theme of the conference was Practical Christianity. We had lectures on Mature Manhood from Dr Biek, one of the American missionaries from Wora-Wora Hospital, and Christian Friendship and Marriage from the Reverend Agbola, the headmaster of the secondary school at Hohoe.

Sam Woode, the SCM travelling secretary, also came to the conference, and stayed with us on Sunday evening on his way back to Cape Coast. As he arrived he told us he had hit a hawk on the road with his car. He said he had put it in the boot of his car. As he opened the boot to show us, the bird sat up and looked ready for flight. He slammed the boot shut again. He intended to eat it!

Dr Binder has been transferred from Ho hospital to Achimota so I am now under the care of Dr Sharkozy, a Hungarian gynaecologist who left his country in the uprising of 1956.

We still have your last year's Christmas card stuck on the living room door as we like it very much. The SCM were here just now to sing carols in place of our usual discussion, so when they asked for *In the bleak midwinter,* we pointed it out to them. A fortnight ago we gave them a talk on Britain to round off our series on other countries. Many students think Britain is a paradise and want to leave Ghana as soon as they can. We pointed out some of the problems of our society as well as its affluence: the ugliness of too much industry, beautiful landscape lost in housing development, and the problems of living in towns: old age, loneliness, delinquency, people without homes and jobs etc.

We recently dispatched a parcel containing some Ghanaian food for you to taste.

Groundnut soup By soup a Ghanaian means something he can pour over his rice, or put his kenke or yam in. I suggest you pour this over rice or potatoes.

Kontomle These are the leaves of cocoyam. We use them rather like spinach.

Beans These are a Mawuli School favourite, mixed with gari (dried cassava – like sawdust), or fried plantain. I always enjoy it when I am on duty. It would probably go best with cold meat or fried eggs and potatoes or chips. But don't imagine tender succulent baked beans or you will be disappointed. We have not tried the tinned ones ourselves, but boil our own as they are much cheaper.

News not written in a letter home: On Easter Saturday 13 April Celia felt labour pains strengthening in the early hours of the morning. Richard went out into the night to find Sam at his house. [Sam was the houseboy we employed for our second year because we had sent John to school at Mawuli] Richard asked him to fetch the doctor who had agreed to collect us and take us to the hospital. Sam arrived at our house about half-an-hour later.

"The doctor has gone hunting," he told us, "and he will not be back for five days." "But don't worry, he said, seeing our faces, "I have told a man."

"What kind of man?" Richard asked.

"He was driving a lorry" was the not very comforting reply.

Because we did not have Sam's faith in the bush telegraph we were very surprised that Doctor Sharkozy arrived about an hour later. He said, "The baby is probably joking."

But when he had examined Celia he said, "The baby is not joking."

So he packed us into his car and drove at speed to the hospital. Because the attempted coup had been carried out by soldiers from Ho Barracks there was a ring of steel around the town. On every road out there was a roadblock with machine guns pointing inwards at approaching vehicles. Dr Sharkozy did not slow down but put his hand on the horn and drove through. We dived to the floor in the back of the car expecting to be raked with gunfire. Later we thought he had probably told them he was attending an emergency when he came through to our home.

Duncan Kwame was born a few hours later. His blue eyes were especially attractive to the Ghanaian ladies and girls who visited him. All boys born in Ghana on a Saturday are called Kwame.

A mother to her child to be born

Feet formed, eyes seeing darkness
Ready
to be born.
Half part shaped of me
Mine
DNA moulded you
Me

The wind promises seeking that which was here
assuring what follows will not change.
The day lilies young as springtime is near
bow to the sun in the morning.

What am I that your feet are me?
What do your eyes see?

In the limp, in the lack;
In the mould of a leper's skin fester;
In the searing pain of born eyes
Seeing.

From the truth of the womb
to the true world
Really.

O mind all-seeing love of God,
What is is what you see.

The breeze leads and the flower dies.
The stream swirls and the rocks decay.
Child to father, a mother cries
and bows to the sun in the morning.

April 1968

Leaving Ho Hospital with Duncan Kwame.

Dr Plewinski is behind. He was a Polish doctor, whose English he had asked us, and we had tried, to improve; though he often told us we were incorrect!

Mawuli – 29 June 1968

Thank you for your letter. We are glad that we can come. We hope to arrive in Hove sometime on the evening of 19 August. We don't know yet whether it will be by train or the car which Mr Norsworthy is kindly lending us.

Early Friday morning Mrs Cudjoe, the wife of the geography teacher who is one of our neighbours, gave birth to a daughter. This is the eighth addition to the Mawuli family this year, and Mrs Diehl's baby is expected within the next two weeks. Kathy Stouffer and I are going to visit Mrs Cudjoe and Afua in the hospital this afternoon.

This is the rainy season, although it is now a hot sunny afternoon. It began to rain at 8.10 yesterday evening and rained hard well into the night. It cut short the treasure hunt Richard and John Stouffer had arranged for the SCM farewell party. The students were divided into four teams and were dashing about the compound making a collection of items. Marks were awarded in proportion to the difficulty of obtaining the article. E.g. a whole piece of chalk or a frangipani blossom two marks, a coconut five, a live invertebrate more than 2 in. long, 10, and an elephant tusk (with or without elephant), 50. We also played a newspaper game, sang, ate Sloppy Joe's (meat sauce over hamburger buns) and cake, and danced Mairi's Wedding. The students presented us each with a pair of kente sandals as a leaving gift.

Richard arrived back from Accra at 7 pm, just in time for the party. He had been to collect our air tickets, and those for some other members of staff. The Ministry of Education will not send them through the post. They must be collected by someone authorised by the head of the school. He is feeling the effects of the journey today and is at present convalescing on the sofa so that he will be well enough to go to the Stouffers for supper and Bridge tonight.

We have a holiday on Monday. I have to take Kwame to the Child Welfare Clinic at the Paramount Chief's house for his smallpox vaccination, otherwise he won't be allowed into Britain. Exams begin on Tuesday.

We have 5 cantaloupe melons in the garden and hope to eat two or three of them before we leave. We harvested our bananas this week and soon we shall pull the ground nuts.

[These letters omit many events: the occasion Richard spoke on Ghana Radio about some lights that had been seen moving in the sky. People were fearful that Nkrumah was returning; his talk at Ola (Roman Catholic) Girls' School, for Education Day, and his working there in the 2nd year with the O level students. There is no description of the day of the Attempted Coup led by soldiers from Ho barracks. We do not have the letters Celia wrote to her parents about her pregnancy, nor how Duncan was born on Easter Saturday, in the holidays, with the result that she missed no teaching. We have not got the letter Celia wrote about the occasion we went in the dark at 4.00 am into Ho for the enstooling of a new Paramount Chief. We were guests of honour and sat in armchairs in the centre of a large space – a goat was sacrificed right in front of us.

But what we have is probably enough to give the reader a taste of our time in Ghana.]

Return to England

We returned from Ghana to find that Richard's brother Andrew was manager of Hatchett's, a restaurant in Piccadilly. We visited once and found him amongst waitresses clad in scanty silver costumes. Everything was silvery including a grand piano. Richard found it disturbing and wrote the following poem:-

Canned Chicken

Chicks that live in runs of steel
choose a house to shelter minds
from the wind, whose power presses
folded wings, and coverts stresses,
setting free the love that binds.

Air is flame that sears the pinions
of the chicken, now untinned;
Left his pecking, can aspire
to love which freedom wins through fire,
and launch himself upon the wind.

Richard taught physics at Eltham Green Comprehensive School in Inner London. Celia was able to give home tuition to children unable to attend school, at our home in Barnehurst, Kent. Justin was born in 1969.

Eltham Green Comprehensive School was a purpose-built comprehensive 7 storeys high with 2300 students and a 14 form entry. Because the Inner London Education Authority operated grammar schools it was not truly comprehensive. It had a small sixth-form. Richard was one of 4 physics teachers. After the 5th and 6th form teaching in Ghana he was now teaching physics and chemistry to the first two years and physics in the 3rd and 4th. Having so many students in the school made it impossible to know them all. The corridors had doors at either end (for safety reasons) but this made discipline impossible outside the classroom. A misbehaving student just ran out of the other end of the corridor confident that the teacher did not know his name and would not catch him (or her).

One of the classes Richard taught in his first year was 2C4, the lowest of the second year (year 8 nowadays) bottom of the C stream and therefore 14th stream. The students were not used to behaving themselves at home or school, had extremely poor numeracy and literacy abilities. After much learning by Richard but none by the children, he learned to write a few lines on the black-board, before the class, which the students copied into their books immediately on arrival. Richard could then concentrate on making sure they did that task. The youngsters quite enjoyed copying. It was not education. It was survival. Eventually Richard was sometimes able to tell them what they had copied and what it meant.

Other classes were not as bad but he had to have his wits about him; to make sure that nothing went out of the window on to *bomb alley* below, everything was collected in and counted when there had been practical work, and that there was no bodily harm being endured by any of the students.

One particular friend Les Hooper also taught physics. He and Richard often taught same year students in adjacent laboratories. Les, being a year ahead in experience of the school, was very helpful to Richard when he first arrived. They operated a policy of sending each other disruptive students without warning. The receiving teacher gave their visitor a very strict time.

Les and Richard also did more positive things. They both coached hockey teams. They started a weekly school newspaper staffed by 4th year students from their teaching groups, each producing a newspaper every other week. The idea was to improve knowledge of what the students were doing. Without it nobody knew about sports results, or about extramural activities undertaken by other youngsters. Richard taught a big Afro-Carribean lad who was a champion at judo in London, but nobody knew until we ran an article about him. The newspaper was called Quaggy, the name of the stream which flowed past the school. It was a convenient name because the Q pigeonhole was always empty in the staffroom and was used by staff to put in information or articles for the paper.

Richard and Les took their 4th year physics groups out on the North Downs on some Saturdays and did some simple orienteering with them. Some had never been in the countryside before.

Richard also ran a chess club which met every week after school and competed in the Times Chess Competition as well as a local competition. Richard was amazed at how compliant and helpful the students were in the chess club. One evening Richard challenged the other school's member of staff to a game. He discovered after he had lost quickly and roundly that he had played Robert G Wade, who had just won the British Chess Championship at Hastings.

Richard did not have much respect for the head teacher. He was unapproachable. Teachers had to make an appointment to see his secretary. He referred to his staff by number on the tannoy, which had an outlet in every room. (Richard was 83) He believed that caning was the best way of dealing with every misdemeanour. One evening after chess club Richard found two young boys breaking the doors off lockers in the corridor. They were not members of his club and he didn't know their names so he was surprised that they didn't run away when he called them to him. He took them down to the room where he knew the Head teacher was having a meeting. He knocked on the door, received no answer and stepped into the room. To his surprise nobody took any notice of him. After a while the head teacher looked up and said, "How dare you interrupt our meeting?" Richard apologised, left, and told the boys they could go. He decided at that point to leave the school at the first opportunity.

We moved to New Milton in 1971 when Richard was appointed a physics teacher at Brockenhurst Sixth-Form College.

Family Life

Normally people only get one chance to be parents. There is no chance to practice and no qualifications they can get in advance. Indeed, since it is the most important job we ever have it is surprising that it forms little or no part of the education system. We were very keen to do the job well. Duncan was such a placid child that we thought of ourselves as excellent parents. But Justin was far more challenging and we soon discovered that we had much to learn.

We believed that television was too materialistic and non-interactive. So we were one of few families in the UK not to have a TV. We tried to spend time with our children, to explore the natural world with them, to play musical instruments together, to go on walks together, and camping expeditions to various wild places in the UK. Each evening we held family prayers and eventually read the whole of a Children's Bible together.

The decision not to have a TV was put under pressure by our boys who felt that they were missing out in conversations at school. It was ended when Richard, at the beginning of the football season, promised that we would get a TV if Southampton were in the FA Cup Final. He thought the promise was safe but the 1976 FA Cup Final took place on 1 May 1976 at Wembley Stadium. It was contested between Manchester United and Southampton. United had finished third in the First Division that season, and were strong favourites, while unfancied Southampton had finished sixth in the Second Division. In one of the biggest shocks in the history of the final,

Southampton won 1–0 through an 83rd-minute goal from Bobby Stokes. It was the first time Southampton had won a major trophy, and they have yet to add any other major honours to their name. It was good to watch the match on our new TV.

The Peter Pan railway, a fairground attraction for children, was an example of what we tried to avoid. Brightly coloured railway engines ran on a small track. Children could ride in them. There was a steering wheel which made no difference to where the engines went. The occupants were just passengers. There was no need for thought, no opportunity for imagination or creativity. We felt that many children's toys were like that. Sometimes they were very expensive, intricate and at first sight interesting, but they had no scope for the child to put in any input, except to break them. We gave the boys wooden blocks to play with when they were young which gave scope for imagination. They had Lego including a railway they could build. Sometimes we operated a railway timetable carrying goods from one room to another in our bungalow.

We supported them by attending football and rugby matches and cross-country running, but when we became very busy, in the term time at Culverley Boarding House, and later, with the youth club at church, our attention to them as individuals suffered. They had some good holidays, with Richard's sister's daughters, skiing, youth hostelling and staying in Cornwall. We back-packed and camped in Snowdonia in the snow when they were very young, and in the Lake District when they were older. We took our camper to the Outer Hebrides and Shetland and gave them experiences of mountains and wild places, of streams and woods. We went out at night once to watch badgers in the New Forest.

One day the Head of PE, Peter Daines, asked the teaching staff if anyone could help by driving the college minibus to Hereford with students going canoeing on the River Wye. Richard volunteered and Pete said that Celia could bring the boys. They could stay in his caravan in the same field as the canoeists. After that Richard and sometimes the rest of the family assisted Pete with running camps in the summer. Sometimes they were just canoeing and the tents were moved down the river gradually from Hay to Mordiford. Sometimes it was a standing camp and the youngsters, including Scandinavian or Dutch boy and girl scouts, canoed, hiked, caved, pony-trekked etc. At first our boys were sometimes left behind as it was term time. They were looked after by Pete's wife Madge, and Celia was able to come to Hereford. For the camps in the school holidays our boys became more competent at handling the canoes as they got older.

One of the difficulties for parents is to get the balance right – between encouragement and criticism, between their children being looked after, and taking responsibility for themselves. We wanted our sons to be self-reliant, to be able to explore and take initiative. We wanted them to do well at school academically as well as in extra-curricular activities. We certainly didn't get it right all the time – but we tried.

We attended St Peter's Church, Ashley. The main activities seemed to be the summer fête and the Christmas fair which we did not value, as they occupied a great deal of time and in our view distracted people from more Christian activities.

We founded a Fellowship Group of about a dozen people and studied material produced by the Post-Green Community in Dorset. We began to grow spiritually ourselves and to think about our own future. Then we were appointed houseparents at a local authority boarding house in Brockenhurst.

Culverley

While Richard remained a full-time physics teacher at Brockenhurst Sixth-form College in Hampshire, for four years, from January 1974 to December 1977, Celia and he were houseparents in charge of Culverley Boarding House. So we were responsible for the welfare of 40 boys aged 11 to 18 who attended 2 comprehensive schools and the college. Richard was determined that it would be nothing like his own boarding school experience. We found a great amount of bullying, and the work of duties in the house was borne almost entirely by the first years. We resolved to share out the work more fairly but had to be very tough to make sure that our instructions were obeyed.

Richard remembers telling the first year lads that the following year some of the first year work would be done by second years. They cheered loudly until one of the brighter ones realised that they would be second years then.

We had to be resolute in various areas. When we arrived Richard complained that the single hand bell was not sufficient as a fire alarm. Richard was told by Hampshire Education Authority that it was adequate. Within a year, however, the local authority arrived with a plan to put in fire escapes, an electric fire-alarm and divide the lovely building into two across its main polished wood staircase. We drew up alternative and (we thought) much better plans for safe alert and escape, and preserve the building as a home. Thankfully we won the argument.

The local authority rules stated that boys were not allowed in the kitchen. To us the chef was a really important listener and critic. We felt it was important that the boys could come into the kitchen on their return from school and tell him how the world was mistreating them. He normally listened to them, helped them to get things into perspective, and gave them a little job helping him.

We inherited a system called "gardening" on Saturday mornings. However it had started it had become an institutionalised bullying regime. The decision as to what jobs were done was left to the senior boy on duty. The other seniors lazed in their rooms. We decided to make the jobs worthwhile and involve all the boys in the house for a shorter time. So we made a vegetable plot. We kept 28 chickens in a house and run made by the boys. They laid 10,000 eggs in 2 years and were fed entirely on scraps from the kitchen and what the hens could forage in the grounds.

Richard was much criticised by some of the older boys for not using corporal punishment on the younger ones. He told them it was not appropriate or necessary. But one night, about 2.00 am we were woken by the door bell. A police officer told us that he had just posted three boys up the fire escape. He just wanted to check that they belonged here and gave me the names of 3 third year boys. They had been trying to break open the cigarette machine in the village. He said he was sure we would know how to deal with them. We thanked him and went back to bed. But Richard was up again a few minutes later. The boys had deliberately broken rules. They knew what they had done was wrong and that they risked punishment. We could punish them with harsh duties and withdrawing privileges in the next days. But Richard decided that because of their deliberate wrong-doing he was not playing his proper part unless they received a short sharp shock that they would remember. So he found a gym shoe, walked down the corridor to their dormitory, called a name and accompanied the lad back to an empty room. He bent over and Richard applied 6 hard hits to his posterior. This was repeated with the other two boys.

The following day there was a different atmosphere in the house. Sadly perhaps Richard had gained a new respect. A few months later he repeated the action for a similar act of wilful wrong-doing. We don't know if we were right or not. Richard told the parents, who supported his decision. They were the only times corporal punishment was used in the house when we were in charge.

We found that the older boys woke up the younger ones when they came to bed. We decided that the Sixth-form boys should have their own study bedrooms and that they should not sleep in the younger boys' dormitories. This was very popular.

Twice, at a two-year interval Richard read the whole of Watership Down [3] to the youngest boys at lights out. He found the accents of the many different animals, challenging. He held a torch to read in the dark dormitory. The book contains 50 short chapters which meant 50 sessions of readings. In the darkness bigger boys including some sixth-formers crept in and listened as well.

We were very keen that the boys should have memorable and life-expanding experiences. We had occasional wide games where teams of boys would spend some hours together in the New Forest trying to achieve an aim. One game was to give all the 30 younger boys a safety match and tell them that their objective was to enter a gravel pit while the 10 oldest boys were guards who were not allowed in the pit but had to catch the younger ones outside it and remove the match from them. This was on a dark November evening. If the younger ones managed to get into the pit with their match they could light a firework rocket. Five of the first years huddled on the edge of a ditch together and waited for the game to end. The other one crawled through several yards of gorse bush and succeeded in entering the gravel pit with his match and sending off a rocket. He was badly scratched but triumphant. Fortunately we did not have to return him to his parents for a month! Not all these games were popular at the time but afterwards they were the source of many reminiscences.

We had the rule that in non-organised time the boys were allowed to watch what TV they liked. The rule was that they had to know what they were watching and when it ended. Newspapers were available in the house but it was surprising how many boys could not be bothered to look in the paper and so did something else. The TV room was often empty. But one dark Friday evening in January Richard watched a lot of boys troop into the room after dinner. He went to the College minibus which lived with us and was available for our use at weekends. He put a mattress across the back of the front seats and dark paper across the outside of the rear windows. Then he went to the TV room.

They had switched on the TV and, as Richard had guessed, no-one in the room knew what they were watching. So Richard told them to put on shoes and a coat and get in the minibus. They could not see out. He drove them for a few miles into the forest making various false turns and stops to confuse them. Then he stopped on a forest track, gave two of them a magnetic compass (but no map) and told them to get back to Culverley as soon as they could. If they failed to get back by 10.00 pm they could find a phone and ring him. All the boys were sent out from different places, in pairs. The first boys were back at the house before him. Only one pair had to be collected having set off in totally the wrong direction and failed to discover their error.

We ran a scheme we called the Culverley Proficiency Certificate. Many of the youngsters lived in the holidays with their families in camps for Armed Service Personnel. They tended to be very good at sport but lacking in experience and self-reliance. Gaining the certificate involved succeeding at a whole range of tasks depending on their age. It might be sitting on their own in silence outside for an hour; with a friend lighting a fire and cooking a simple meal in the open air; making a balsa wood or plastic model; making a return bus journey having looked up the times in a timetable. Another task was to go as a pair for a weekend camp in a New Forest campsite, walking the five miles there carrying tent, food and other gear. We emphasised that they should prepare things themselves and clean up afterwards. One pair of youngsters failed to label the cooking oil or washing up liquid. They said the fried eggs had tasted awful!

Windows were always being broken. We held the view that no voices would be raised nor would there be criticism. Accidents happen. But the breaker also had to be the repairer. If the lad was young a sympathetic older boy was asked to help. The new glass could be bought from the village iron-monger but it had to be measured by the boy. The cost was put on the Culverley account. Several times a piece of glass was brought back which went clean through the hole. The iron-monger kindly allowed it to be returned in exchange for a new piece of appropriate size. We didn't think they got away without a little teasing!

Celia and Richard were in loco parentis. This was quite strenuous at parents' evenings at the schools. We had 6 children in each year group. We used the lads to reserve places in queues and moved swiftly from teacher to teacher. It was probably helpful that we were teachers ourselves.

Previous to our rule the boys had been told that they were not allowed girl friends or even boy friends from the village. We allowed them to have friends who we tried to take an interest in. For a year we even had a music group with one of our lads and 3 from outside who practised diligently and incessantly some weekends. We can still call to mind the repetitive rhythm of one of the songs they had written. There was a tradition of a party before Christmas to which they were allowed to invite a girl each. The last words to us of our predecessor were, "Under no circumstances allow a Christmas party!" At the party the previous year large quantities of alcoholic drink (which was not allowed) were smuggled in and there had been drunkenness.

Fortunately, we had a year to think about this. We held conversations with the older boys and eventually decided on the following rules. No-one was to bring alcohol into the house. If they did the punishment would be severe. But we would have a free bar. There would be no spirits but beer, lager and cider would be available as well as soft drinks depending on the age of the youngsters. The older lads were at first suspicious but we discussed which drinks and what quantities.

We decided to distract the boys and so decided that the party would have a theme. It was to be undersea so in the weeks before the end of the Christmas term a wreck was constructed in the largest dormitory, big enough to get into and eat in. 400 fish and fathoms of seaweed were cut out and coloured. A huge anchor was made, and coloured lights set up. It looked good and we had a great party with no problems at all.

There were 3 more successful parties in our 4 years. The only one with trouble had a Western theme. Richard met one of the girls at the front door – a 15 year old. She had consumed much of a bottle of wine on the train and was plainly drunk. Richard phoned her parents and invited them to fetch her without allowing her inside the house. At the same party one of the sixth-form boys decided to ignore the instruction not to drink too much. We had borrowed 30 large straw bales from a farm about three-quarters of a mile up the road. Over the next two days he took them all back in a wheel barrow on his own to help him to recover.

One amusing incident occurred just before one of the parties. We had invited a Salvation Army Officer to talk to the boys about life in community as part of a series for the 3rd and 4th years. After his talk he came back with us to our flat. He had laid the dangers of drink on thickly to the boys and continued with the same theme to us. We were so glad when he left without asking for the toilet. If he had gone upstairs he would have found on the landing many crates of beer ready for the party.

We decided to leave Culverley and return to New Milton when our own boys were approaching the age of the boys in the house. We felt their loyalties would be stretched.

While we were at Culverley we bought a VW Camper as a vehicle to escape from the house in the holidays. Our first trip in May 1975 was to Wales, to a valley in the mountains north of Abergavenny where we camped wild, by a stream. Richard wrote these poems; the first when we were there and the second on our return home.

Man and Stream

I have decided,
sitting on a rock,
to plan –
representative of my race,
shaper and engineer –
what can be done with this stream.

And I notice –
observation my first tool –
the undisciplined power and ceaseless repetition
of its motion.

Now purpose –
To encompass the stream
in the mind
of man –
conveyor of waste or materials;
provider of energy
or refreshment.

The grey rocks
lack scope
because
they are irregular
and difficult
to extract.

A child may play
and learn
something
of texture, grasp
and shape;
but then
the transport problems
of children
or rocks
in adequate numbers –
to say nothing
of safety codes to cover all eventualities.

The water,
swirling,
sprinkles the sunshine;
the sound of its tumbling
induces
peace.

It may be the wind in the grass
and heather purple rocks
and the wild potency of water
can shape the maker
and mould
him;
but to what possible socio-economic benefit?

30 May 1975

I can remember a bright young valley
with a redstart gentling his welcome
by a sandstone wall.
We camped near a stream,
optimistic from the mountain,
eager and rock-tumbling
between alders and white rowans.

Fresh in my mind
is the joy of our clambering,
stone-stepping the stream with symmetrical fern
and rock-moss glistening like mica.
We stopped to admire a self-confident flycatcher,
dappled and sure in the subtlety of colour,
and almost trod on a pipit's nest
with five dark eggs
in the high and windy tussock land
where sheep and ponies were grazing.

What have I lost in the green morning
with cuckoo's bubbling
and ravens and a buzzard soaring above?
Did I imagine or was there a meeting
of me and the valley
in the May sunshine?
A mile of transparencies,
rocks brought home,
love shared among memories,
cannot revive
the youth dead with the sheep skulls
in that short Welsh summer.

The Shetlands

We journeyed to the Shetland Islands in our campervan one summer holiday. The Motorail from Brockenhurst to Stirling left a few hundred yards from Culverley. British Railways sent us a map to help us find the station! It was a bit disconcerting to find that the one advertised as a highly skilled driver putting our vehicle on to the train was one of Richard's A level students! We had sleeper berths overnight on the train. After a night which included a fair amount of banging about we awoke early to find the train speeding through the beautiful valley between the Howgill Fells and the Lake District. From Stirling we drove to Aberdeen and on to a piece of rope netting. The camper was craned up in the air and on to the St Clair.

The 200 mile voyage was overnight and we had cabins. We awoke in the morning as we steamed up the east side of Shetland Mainland. Arriving in Lerwick we stayed with some friends from University who had lived in the Outer Hebrides but moved to Shetland. He was a teacher. They lived near Sandwick further south.

We travelled all over the islands, staying in our camper. One expedition was to the very north, to Hermaness on Unst. We walked along the headland following guide posts in the fog. On either side were three hundred foot (100 metres) cliffs down to the sea.

The boys exchanged a glove

At one point the fog was so thick we had to use ourselves as guide posts to find the next one. To make it even more atmospheric Great Skuas kept emerging from the murk just by us, and then vanishing again. Our boys worked out that we were distinguishing them by their differently coloured gloves, as the rest of their kit was similar. So they exchanged a glove to make it more difficult for us!

As we looked down at the end of the headland on to Muckle Flugga, the fog lifted and we could see the rock with its lighthouse below. The sun came out and we realised we were close to dozens of puffins with their brightly coloured beaks.

Muckle Flugga is the most northerly rock in the British Isles. A temporary lighthouse was established and first lighted on 11 October 1854. The light sits on a jagged outcrop of skerries a mile north of Unst and right in the path of the Atlantic storms. It was first named "North Unst" but changed in 1964 to Muckle Flugga.

The temporary lighthouse building is said to have been completed in 26 days. As the structure itself (50ft - 15 metres in height) was on rock 200ft (60m) above sea level it was thought that it would have to withstand only the wind and the rain. However, when the winter gales began to attack the rock it was found that the sea not only broke heavily on the tower, but ran up the sides and burst open the door of the dwelling room on top. A 64 foot (20m) high brick tower was built, with foundations sunk ten feet (3m) into the rock, and a permanent light appeared on 1 January 1858.

The work was designed and supervised by brothers David and Thomas Stevenson of the famous family of lighthouse builders[4]. They were sons of Robert, the father of the dynasty. Robert Louis, who preferred being a writer to life as an engineer, was Thomas' son.

Back in Sandwick we took a boat trip to the uninhabited island of Mousa and visited the best preserved broch in the UK. It is a 2000 year old fort, even today over 13m tall, little short of its original height. This magnificent building stands on a rocky headland on the west coast of Mousa. It is of dry stone construction. The tower's diameter is 15m at the base, tapering to 12m at the top. There is only one narrow entrance. The walls are 4.5m thick, with a stone stair rising spirally inside the wall, lit by vertical gaps in the inner broch's face. We climbed up to the top and enjoyed a splendid view over the Sound of Mousa.

We found a horse mushroom big enough to fill a frying pan and carried it triumphantly back to Sandwick.

One day we journeyed to the west and met a couple crofting by a sea loch near Walls. They were digging peat for the winter so we helped them stack it so it would dry. They had a simple lifestyle which we admired.

Another day we went with our friends and their children to a headland to the west of Sandwick. While the children were playing on the beach their bright orange and black football was thrown into the sea. The breeze immediately took it away from the shore. It was too quick for us. I ran round to some rocks which it was going to pass close to but it was well out of my reach.

It was time to go home. We drove up the steep road from the beach on top of the cliffs. Through binoculars we could see the ball still sailing to the east. Somebody said, "It's going home."

When we arrived back at our friends' home we rushed down to the beach. Right in the centre of the white sand was the shiny orange and black ball. It had travelled safely about 2 miles across the sea and got there before us.

On our journey back on the St Clair the vehicle was again hoisted aboard. It was spinning round and bumped the side of the vessel. Fortunately no serious damage was done. It was put very high up on the ship. The journey through the Pentland Firth was rough though there was thick fog off Aberdeen so we anchored for 5 hours offshore. When we disembarked we found the green campervan white with salt sprayed on by the wind. We found a car wash in the city to renew its bright and shiny look.

Outer Hebrides

On another expedition, in August 1979, we enjoyed several weeks holiday in our campervan on the Outer Hebrides. We sailed from Oban through the Sound of Mull to South Uist. Straight off the ferry in Lochboisdale we tried to turn round by backing on to some fresh green sward. Sadly it was weed on a deep water-filled ditch. A local inhabitant spotted us and arrived rapidly and pulled us out with his vehicle.

We enjoyed several days camping on the machair, walking and watching birds. The wild flowers were amazingly colourful and profuse. The water we carried in our tank soon ran out and we got some more from a stream. But it was stained brown from the peat and didn't look inviting. Richard wasn't feeling too well so Celia took the lads to a nearby croft and asked for water. It was the owner's birthday and a party was in progress to which they were invited. After a little while of conversation Celia said that her husband wasn't well and she should return to the camper. The crofter went to the tap in the kitchen with our 1 gallon containers and returned with them full to the brim with very brown water!

After a few more days we drove to North Uist across the smaller island of Benbecula, changing the laid back, untidy, Catholic South for the more manicured Protestant north. From the north coast there is a prominent headland. We noticed that a track was marked on the map across the beach from the road to the headland. It was only available at low water. We decided to drive across and camp on the headland.

There was no actual track so we estimated where it was intended, and when the tide was out, drove off the road on to the wide expanse of sand. It was like driving across Bonneville Salt Flats and we went at a good speed. We weren't sure where the track was meant to go on the headland so we chose a likely looking spot and drove straight into some loose sand. For a moment the wheels spun – then half the wheels were covered in sand as the vehicle bedded down, and we were stuck. We got out to survey the situation. There was no drift wood or anything else we could wedge under the wheels. What could we do?

We were several miles from the nearest road. Of course there was no phone in the days before mobiles. We had a few hours before the sea would return. The sand we were stuck in was quite loose so we thought/hoped that the tide would not come in this far. In those days we used to talk about "arrow prayers" – quick darts of prayer to God. We sent up a short arrow – HELP!

Immediately, around the corner of the headland appeared a tractor which came towards us. Richard bounced towards it and asked the driver if he could kindly pull us out of our trouble. He said nothing but backed up the tractor to the campervan and waited patiently.

"Have you got a rope?" he asked.

"I hoped you might have one," Richard replied.

"I'll have one back at my house," he said, and drove off.

Soon he was a dot in the distance. It was a long way to the road and presumably even further to where he lived. Would he return?

He did: first as a dot, eventually as a tractor backing up to our vehicle. He pulled us onto the firm sand and suggested that we use the track which everybody else used which he had just come down! We were so grateful. We offered him money and a box of chocolates, but he would accept nothing.

We spent a few days on the headland. A Swiss couple in a tent were camping there too. They were hoping to see big waves but were disappointed.

Eventually it was time to move on. We left the headland, drove successfully across the beach, and travelled along the narrow road to Lochmaddy. We embarked on the little ferry to Tarbert on the Isle of Harris – the name Tarbert, from the Norse, indicating a narrow isthmus which the Vikings may have used to drag their boats across.

Running down the dunes before falling in a heap of laughter

We then camped near the beach by Valtos on the edge of the sea-loch Roag on the North-West side of the Isle of Lewis. It was a lovely spot and there were huge sand dunes which our boys enjoyed running down, falling over in a heap of laughter at the base. One calm day we got out our little inflatable dinghy, and having careful regard to the tides, paddled across to the island called Pabay Mor. We could see deep down in the crystal clear water the sea anemones and crabs on the seabed.

Celia and Duncan with Pabay Mor in the distance

The island was cleared for sheep in 1824 and was now uninhabited. We pulled the dinghy (which we called Puffer) up on the beach and explored part of the island. We found the remains of houses and a chapel and tried to imagine what it was like living in this remote place.

After some weeks of exploring the Outer Hebrides we reached Lionel at the Northern tip of the Isle of Lewis and stayed for a few days with the same friends we had visited on the Shetland Islands. They had now returned to Lewis.

There was great excitement because the Queen was coming to Stornoway. We were up early, travelled down from Lionel, and took our places amongst the small crowd on the quay. The

Royal Yacht Britannia was visible through the drizzle, out in the bay. A Royal Barge left the Royal Yacht and began the trip towards us.

Meanwhile a squad of soldiers began to form up. Their sergeant inspected them. Sometimes he lifted a cap, flattened their hair and replaced the cap. We could hear hammering from below the quay at the pontoon where Her Majesty was to arrive. This seemed to be leaving things a bit late!

The Royal Barge drew closer and eventually went out of our sight below the quay. The carpenter with his bag of tools emerged from the steps – just in time. Surely Prince Phillip had noticed him.

Then a man walked swiftly out of the nearby office carrying a large roll of red carpet. The end was draped down in front of him – too low. He trod on the end – unfortunately in a puddle – and just stopped himself from falling over. He rolled out the carpet from the top of the steps in front of the soldiers. And there right at the end was a large dirty wet mark. For a moment there was consternation. The Royal Barge was at the platform and the royal party was disembarking.

And then the man who had been carrying the carpet re-emerged with a huge pair of scissors. He ran to the end of the carpet, and with a couple of strokes snipped off the final metre. He disappeared just as the Queen rose on to the quay. She was serene, and there was no sign that she was aware of the commotion preceding her advent.

There was much flag-waving and cheering. She inspected the soldiers and seemed satisfied with their caps and hair. She graciously accepted the two fine lobsters presented to her.

Back to New Milton

At Christmas 1977 we left Culverley and returned to our bungalow in New Milton. Duncan was now 9 and Justin 8. We decided that it would have tested their loyalties too much to be the same age as boys in the boarding house.

We returned to St Peter's Church, Ashley and met Chris and Sue Herman. We teamed up with them in running a youth fellowship. We encouraged the youngsters to take part in the church, and ran activities for them at weekends and on Sunday evenings. We camped with them at Hillfield Friary in Dorset several times and one year made a short Christian adventure video film with them. Chris and Sue came to the Fellowship Group which gave it a new spirit of life.

We invited church members to come to events such as a performance of a Christian musical play with an entertainer named Ishmael (Ian Smale), backed up by the church youngsters. We also encouraged the children to take part in church activities – even the summer fête which we had no success in removing from the church programme.

We took the children to Brownsea Island in Poole harbour and cycling in the New Forest and on the Isle of Wight, as well as doing many other things with them.

Our two-bedroom bungalow was not really big enough for us. The boys, who had been sharing a room, needed separate bedrooms. So we built an upstairs. Pete Daines, (the canoeist) suggested that we did not need to employ a building firm. We could do some of the work ourselves and employ tradesmen for the things we could not manage. So Celia drew the plans. The whole family were involved in the design. On the first day the plumber did not arrive. We rang him to be told that he wasn't well and if Richard were any kind of physics teacher he should be able to disconnect the water tank himself! So he did.

The carpenter did most of the work with us holding the other end of the wood and passing tiles down and timber up. Richard rewired the house. Celia and Richard did the painting and decorating. It was a good summer vacation. We had a firm to supply and fit new hardwood window frames. The only major mistake was that they measured incorrectly so that none of the double-glazed units would fit in the frames. They all had to be replaced, which left us a bit draughty for a few weeks.

With Richard teaching at the college, Celia doing home tuition, both working with the young people and the Fellowship Group, growing many of our own vegetables, and exploring wildlife and the New Forest with our sons, as well as supporting them in their music and sport, we were very busy.

A visit from an otter

"Very quietly, come here" Richard called Celia.

Gently she came and stood on the rock in the stream on which he was standing. Together they looked perhaps 50 metres down the beck. They could see the arching back of an otter glistening in the sun as it dived and swam towards them.

Celia had been cooking the evening meal outside their little tent a few yards away.

Only a few weeks before in July 1982, Richard had been travelling on a train to his work as a teacher at Brockenhurst Sixth-form College. He had been given a questionnaire to fill in about the journey: Where did he get on? Where was he going? What was the purpose of his journey? He was only 8 minutes on the train and hardly registered that there was a prize for one traveller at each station as he put the completed paper in an oil drum on the platform. So it was a surprise when, a few weeks later, in the summer vacation, one of the Senior Tutors arrived at his house with the instruction to phone British Railways. He had not put his address on the paper, only his name and where he worked. But the railway official had taken the trouble to phone the college, and the Senior Tutor, in college to guide students after their A-level results, had kindly brought the news to New Milton on his way home. Richard had been picked out to receive two first class return tickets to anywhere on the UK mainland.

"Where do you wish to travel to?" said the voice.

"Do I have to say now?"

"Yes"

A quick glance at the atlas and then "The Kyle of Lochalsh, please"

Duncan and Justin were to be away on Scout camp on the Isle of Wight for a week and so there would be an opportunity to use the free tickets very soon. But a quick look at the timetables showed that the Kyle of Lochalsh, the station at the end of the line on the way to the Isle of Skye, was out of range for a week unless we were to spend the whole time travelling.

We decided to go to Penrith on the train and then walk up the Roman Road called High Street, down to Troutbeck and finally to Bowness-on-Windermere where we would catch the train home.

The morning after the boys had been despatched to camp we caught the train in New Milton and entered a first class compartment. It was quite a crowded train and it was obvious that the only other occupant of our carriage did not believe that these two somewhat scruffy people, with rucksacks and walking boots, had paid for first class tickets. The train sped to Brockenhurst where one of the assistant housemasters at Culverley House, with whom we had worked several years before, got on the train and stood in the corridor outside our compartment. He greeted us by throwing open the door and half singing announced, "I know what you're doing, you haven't got a ticket." And then shut the door again.

91

Soon a ticket collector arrived. He inspected the ticket of the gentleman in his suit, with a briefcase on the seat beside him. He then turned to us. Three people were together surprised that our tickets were in order and the inspector left the compartment shutting the door quietly behind him.

The rest of the journey was uneventful though much enjoyed by our pair of explorers – especially the valley (which we remembered from our Shetland journey - see page 80) past the Howgill Fells after Oxenholme. And so we came to Penrith and at 5.00 pm were transformed from first class train travellers to heavily laden hikers.

We carried food for five days together with a fairly light tent, fairly light sleeping bags; a fairly heavy primus stove with paraffin … The rucksacks seemed quite heavy as we walked up the road from the station to the big roundabout across the M6. Carefully minding the rushing traffic we crossed the A66 and took a footpath to the west under the railway line and across the River Eamont. We came to the village of Sockbridge and up a lane which led us to the track passing Winder Hall Farm.

We decided to camp in the woodland just past the farm but couldn't find anyone to ask permission. We had also hoped they would give us some water for cooking. The upshot was that we drew water from a horse trough hoping it was clean but boiling it well just in case.

We survived, and the following morning continued along the track which the map told us was the course of the Roman Road, High Street. As we ascended we soon caught sight of Ullswater to the west. We continued all day and eventually, searching for a camping place with water, peeled off to the right and followed the course of a beck downwards until there was a small flattish piece of grass on which we pitched our tent. We were tired and it wasn't long before we were asleep.

The following day, Wednesday, was wet. We could hear the rain beating on the flysheet and it continued all day. We read, talked, played games, ate and hoped it would stop. But when we drifted off to sleep it was still pouring.

Thursday was dry but very windy. We decided to go down to Ullswater. So, leaving our tent high on the mountain, we walked down by the stream and enjoyed cheese sandwiches at Howtown Hotel. Then we walked round the southern end of Ullswater to Glenridding. After exploring the town and having a rest, we took a steamer across the lake to Howtown and climbed back up to the tent.

Friday dawned sunny and bright. We continued along High Street, still ascending. Brown Rigg (400m), Loadpot Hill (671m), Wether Hill (670m) passed under our feet on the track where Roman Legionaries had marched so many years ago. After lunch we reached High Raise (802m) where we stood and looked at the reservoir Haweswater far below us to the East. And then we were on the ridge called High Street (828m). Why did the Romans build their road right up here?

It was chilly on top so we didn't spend long looking south over Windermere before we set off again – this time down. Soon High Street was accompanied down the valley by Hagg Gill and then we entered Troutbeck. Just before the track entered farmland we decided to pitch camp.

It was a lovely evening, and it was here, while Celia was cooking the evening meal with some mushrooms we had found, that we saw the otter. Totally still and silent we watched it fishing as it slowly came towards us. We were transfixed as it gave us a better and better view. Soon it was only a few metres away. Was it never going to notice us? And then it was at our feet and put its front paws on the very rock on which we were standing. It was about to haul itself up the rock when it looked up, straight into our faces. It was a moment worthy of a cartoon film. The otter equivalent of a look of horror spread over its whiskered face – and it was gone. Like silver lightning it sped down the stream. We saw its back glistening as it returned the way it had come.

And we ate our meal in the evening sunshine wondering if it could have been true; wondering at our good fortune at gaining a memory that would last all our lives.

The lettercard describing the walk that Celia sent to her parents:

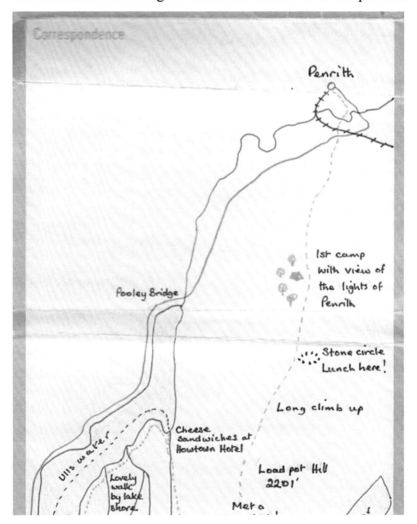

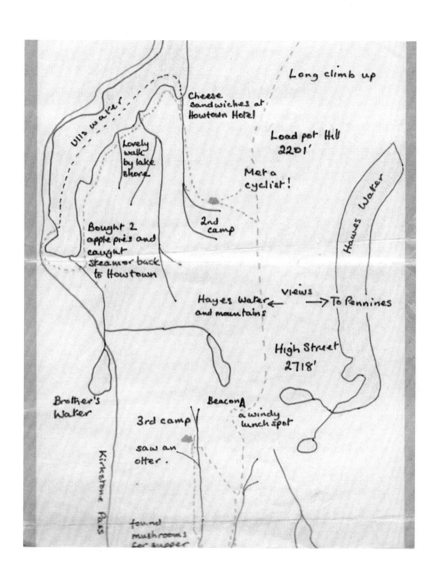

Long climb up

Cheese
sandwiches at
Howtown Hotel

Load pot Hill
2201'

Met a
cyclist!

Ulls water?

Lovely
walk
by lake
shore

2nd
camp

Bought 2
apple pies and
caught
steamer back
to Howtown

Hawes Water

Views

Hayes Water →← → To Pennines
and mountains

High Street
2718'

Brother's
Water

Beacon▲

3rd camp

a windy
lunch spot

saw an
otter.

Kirkstone Pass

found
mushrooms
for supper

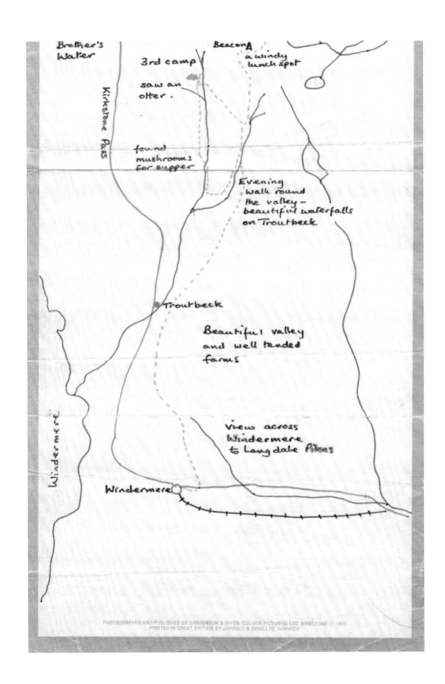

Brother's
Water

Beacon▲
a windy
lunch spot

3rd camp

saw an
otter.

Kirkstone Pass

found
mushrooms
for supper

Evening
walk round
the valley -
beautiful waterfalls
on Troutbeck

●Troutbeck

Beautiful valley
and well tended
farms

Windermere

View across
Windermere
to Langdale Pikes

Windermere○

PHOTOGRAPHED AND PUBLISHED BY SANDERSON & DIXON (COLOUR PICTURES) LTD, AMBLESIDE © 1971
PRINTED IN GREAT BRITAIN BY JARROLD & SONS LTD, NORWICH

Ordained Ministry

We were very busy with college, church and our youngsters. During the early part of 1983 Richard began to feel that God was trying to speak to us but that we were too busy to listen. He got a pain in his neck which really troubled him. The GP put him in a firm collar. He walked out of the surgery and was preparing to cross the road through New Milton when an elderly lady asked if she could assist him. It was more than he could cope with so the collar was thrown away.

We decided to stop attending the church and hand over responsibility for the young people and the Fellowship Group. It was a little extreme but the idea was to spend time in prayer and reading to allow ourselves to hear what God was saying. The boys continued going to church. Chris and Sue picked up our church responsibilities, and we spent time listening to the Lord.

At one point a member of the college teaching staff who was a Christian asked Richard if he ever prayed at night.

"No!" He assured her, "I sleep very well at night."

"Do you ever wake in the night?"

"Never," He assured her.

"Well, if you do wake in the night, ask yourself whether God is asking you to pray," she said.

A few nights later he found to his horror that he was wide awake at 2 o'clock in the morning.

"Hello God," he said. "Goodnight" and he turned over to go to sleep. But he remained awake.

"You can't be serious," he thought. But eventually he got up and crept into the lounge.

The same thing happened for several more nights and he gradually learned that he did not have to speak in prayer. He could listen, and feel wonder and praise – and he learned to speak silently in tongues. It was a strange time and he had no idea what was happening or going to happen. His neck stopped hurting.

Late one evening – on 5 April 1983 – he received a silent but definite word from the Lord which told him to go back into the church and seek ordination. It was actually stronger than that. It was an almost physical command that left him hardly able to speak. God told him he was ordained, and that we should go back into the church. To many people's surprise he never had any doubt that the Anglican Selection Conference which he attended in Chester a year later would recommend him for ordination.

So in August 1984 we moved to Oxford. It was hard to find a property close to Wycliffe Hall, where he was to study, though we were keen to do that. One day we were in an estate agent's in Summertown, north Oxford, when a couple came in to instruct them to sell a small house in Jericho. We snapped it up and sold our house in New Milton.

The Wycliffe Principal, Geoffrey Shaw, was very kind to us. He allowed Celia to join in as much of the programme as she wished, which was most of it. Her essays were marked too, and ultimately she received a special certificate for her efforts. The general rule was that children were allowed to eat in the refectory at lunch-time but not in the evening. Most of the students were much younger than us and their children were pre-school. But our boys were at school in the 4th and 6th years and so could never come to lunch. Geoffrey welcomed them to eat in hall, perhaps weekly he suggested, at dinner. They felt part of the hall and even played occasionally in sports teams.

We left our home in the care of Wycliffe to be used by student-families when we moved in 1986 to Guildford. When we eventually retired and came to sell our Oxford house we were surprised how much it had appreciated in value; enough to buy a house in a wonderful location in Scotland. We praised God for the way he had looked after us in this way.

Before ordination in Guildford Cathedral, those of us about to be ordained held a 4 day pre-ordination retreat at St Columba's House in Woking. There were 15 of us and we were required to keep silent the whole time except when having a personal conversation with the leader, Brother Bernard SSF, Father Guardian of the Anglican Franciscans. He gave us an address each day and then we spent time on our own. On the Friday he called Richard for interview. At one point he picked up a throwaway comment about Richard's own worth. He questioned Richard deeply, and he eventually told Brother Bernard about the hurts of his childhood. Bernard said that Richard had a great number of people to forgive and that on the next day he was not to come to Bernard's talk but spend his time going through his memories and forgiving all those people (possibly including himself) who had hurt him.

It was a lovely sunny day which Richard spent alone in his room. He did exactly as Bernard had said and experienced the most wonderful washing of the Holy Spirit. Most of the day he was in tears and at the end felt exhilarated but completely washed out. In the evening he went into the garden and sat on the grass at the edge of a flower border watching a bumblebee foraging for pollen. Bernard came up behind him and said, "You have been working very hard today. You will find you are more able to minister if you are not carrying all that baggage with you."

Richard served his title (as they say) by becoming Curate of Christ Church, Guildford under the leadership of the Rev. Michael Pain. He was about the same age, and Richard was able to learn a great deal from Michael's example of love and humility.

The study at theological college is theoretical – Biblical Studies, Ethics, Church History etc. Practical things are learned whilst a curate. Some of these things were orderly and planned – others a little more accidental or precipitate. After a few weeks in Guildford, Michael told Richard that he was going on holiday and that Richard would be in charge for 3 weeks. Richard said,

"What about funerals? I know nothing about them."

"Don't worry," said Michael, "nobody will die."

Richard was not re-assured and so there was some discussion as to what Richard should do if there was a funeral.

In the event Michael was wrong. Richard's first funeral was for a still-born boy whose parents, both only children, had no living relative. The parents and Richard were alone in the crematorium with a small white coffin. The main part of the service was sobbing together while hugging the young parents. Amazingly, and sadly, the second funeral, a few days later, was also for a still-born boy. The third, and final one while Michael was away, was for a lecturer from Guildford College who had had a nerve illness which caused him great pain. The man had committed suicide. The funeral service at Guildford Crematorium was attended by hundreds of people, mainly men dressed in black who looked totally blank. The widow had chosen two hymns but Richard was the only one who sang them.

We were well-supported in Guildford by Michael and his wife Angela and by members of the congregation. Both our mothers died while we were there, Celia's very suddenly of an aneurism of the brain, Richard's over several months with cancer. For some weeks his mother received treatment from a radiotherapy machine at a hospital just a few hundred yards from where we lived. Richard was able to pop in at any time. That was the only time he felt that he had anything like a proper son-mother relationship. He thought the strained relationship of the whole of his life became somewhat healed.

We were four years in Guildford and learnt a great deal and made many friends. We were responsible for the older young people, and began a group called 17CC (Aged 17 upwards - CC was Christ Church). We met weekly and also had other activities. We tried to keep the group in touch with those members who were away at University and welcomed them back when they returned for vacations. Those returning were also good at advising those preparing for college – giving them good advice like not shutting their room door when they first arrived, to make contact with others; and possibly colouring their milk green so that others would not use it!

Towards the end of our time there, the heating system in the church building began leaking, and dry rot developed at one side and wet rot at the other. Because Christ Church was a listed building radiators had to be made in a Victorian style which meant that £100,000 had to be found. Michael went on sabbatical leave, saying it would be good experience for Richard to try to raise the money. He went at the task with enthusiasm, with much teaching about giving. He said raising money in this wealthy area was a spiritual problem not a material one. Eventually the church spent one weekend of prayer, worship and giving. We praised God for the £105,000 that was donated or pledged.

Bradley

After 4 years in Guildford it was time to move on to lead a church and parish. We looked at adverts, listened to recommendations and filled in application forms. All Church of England parishes have a patron who is responsible for filling vacancies. For some parishes it is the Diocesan Bishop; for some an independent board of trustees representing a group with a particular theological stance – probably Evangelical or Anglo-Catholic. For many the Crown is the patron and the office administering this work is in 10 Downing Street.

So Richard went to London and was admitted to Downing Street. He had his passport in his pocket but was not required to show it. He approached the door of number 10, wondering if he would have to ring the doorbell, but to his surprise the door opened and he was announced by name. A cabinet meeting had just finished and so he found himself in the hall with many faces he had seen only on television. Geoffrey Howe, John Major, Norman Lamont and Ken Clarke were among those he immediately recognised. He didn't spot Mrs Thatcher. Perhaps she was hiding from the knives that were soon to stab her. He was whisked away to an office deep in the bowels of the earth (The house seemed much bigger on the inside than it looked on the outside), and spoke to a gentleman about benefices in the patronage of the Crown.

In the end he was appointed 13th vicar of St Martin's Church, Bradley in the Black Country, after answering an advert by the Baldwin-Pugh Trustees. Bradley is the place where John Wilkinson chose to build his ironworks in the 18th century. It is to the south-east of Bilston between Wolverhampton and Birmingham. From then until the 1970s, the area had become one of heavy industry, coal-mining and steel-making. We wrote more about this in our first book, Walkers on Water [5]. When we arrived the area was covered in the relics of factories. Many people were unemployed. The Church Centre was being used for courses in painting and decorating, and nursery gardening to help bring hope to some of the unemployed people.

There had been a fine church building with a tall spire that Bradley folk never tired of telling us was a landmark. They could see it from a distance and it told them where home was. Anthropologists call Bradley an urban village – one of many in the Black Country. They are not alluding to thatched cottages round a village green. It is a very urban place. But the people descending from Welsh and Scots and Northern English, whose forbears originally came for work in industry, have developed particular local speech patterns and parochial behaviour. Traditionally the children who went to school together walked to work together and settled down locally. The housing had been poor, built round courtyards with communal toilets and clothes washing facilities. There had been poor diet and ill-health. The children did not usually move away but, often lived with their parents, married or unmarried, or stayed very local. They were mostly practical, hard-working folk, though there were some who did not seek work but lived on state benefits. It was not a pretty area – there were no postcards of Bradley – but the people were proud of it. When they asked, as they did, if we liked Bradley, we said, "We like the people."

Richard's predecessor, the Rev John Brumwell, had been an inspirational man. On his appointment he had to face the knowledge that the church building had been condemned because of dry rot in its roof. And so the church building was demolished in 1974 and the people moved to worship on Sundays in the new Church of England Controlled Primary School at the other end of the parish. Many of the people of the parish blamed John for destroying the church. When Richard arrived in 1990 he knocked on many doors and introduced himself. He was surprised by the anger which often greeted him, "Taking down the church was sacrilege!" Only occasionally did he hear the view expressed by one son of a deceased lady to his brothers and sisters, "What did we do to support it?"

In the school the church flourished. They no longer had the weight of responsibility for a decaying building. And John kept the message simple. He told them the church is not a building – it is the people worshipping God. And he taught mainly from the New Testament. John taught them that a Christian is not someone who goes to church, nor gives money to the church, nor has been christened, nor who used to go to church when they were a child. He said it was someone who had given their life to Christ and was trying to live as his disciple. He quoted 1 Peter 3:15, "In your hearts set apart Christ as Lord. Always be prepared to give an answer to everyone who asks you to give the reason for the hope that you have." And he taught them that they were a family.

John persuaded them to buy the old Church of England school which was next door to where the former church building had been and was rapidly becoming derelict. He wanted a 7 days a week church. He led a team of workers from the increasing congregation in restoring and converting the old school into a building suitable for a church family.

He persuaded them that one of the most important things they could do was to engage in children's and youth work. When he was told that children were the church of the future he said they are part of the church of today. And so the church formed a Church Lads' and Church Girls' Brigade company. Officers were appointed who gave their all to encourage youngsters in the faith. The youngsters were expected to attend Sunday morning communion services every week, and mostly they did. At first many of them were children of those attending church, but gradually children joined whose parents did not attend. An old minibus was bought to collect them from their homes on a Sunday morning. It was used also by the elderly folks Lunch Club which met twice a week in the Church Centre and ate in the old school kitchen. The old school was good for providing a number of rooms for the children to meet in different age-groups.

Richard saw himself as very much standing on John's shoulders.

John had left saying that the church needed new blood and new ideas. One small change Richard wanted to make was the front door. The old door was functional, but only just. It was certainly not good-looking. The door was one thing that was stopping people thinking that the Church Centre was a suitable building in which to hold their wedding or their loved-one's funeral. It seemed to Richard that the church had become very separate from the parish. Apart from an excellent baptism ministry in which lay people followed up children who had been baptised and encouraged them to join the Brigade and come to church, there seemed to be no ways into the church. So the new oak front door was a sign of a new accessibility. The building had been the school for many people approaching the door for the first time. Previously folk were welcomed with the ASB (Alternative Service Book), the Service Book introduced to the Church of England in 1980. It contained many different services, Bible readings and psalms – and was 1200 pages long. Richard thought it a big *turn-off* to those who were not really comfortable with reading and books. Added to this was a hymn book, *With One Voice*, published in Australia in 1977. The church had also begun to use hymns from Mission Praise, a slim text with 282 hymns and songs produced originally in 1984 to accompany Billy Graham's Mission England. Richard was very keen to introduce some of the excellent songs and hymns written since 1984 so sheets of paper and small booklets with these songs in were added to the pile.

The situation was improved with the purchase of a scan printer which enabled the production of service sheets cheaply and quickly. This was accompanied by buying Bibles so the ASB and hymn books were abandoned. The congregation had just a Bible and service sheet in their hands. New hymns and songs could easily be used. Prayers which had been in abstract or difficult language in the service book could be rewritten so that they were relevant, and more straightforward. Inclusive language was used so that the language did not sound as if it only applied to men. These changes took several years to effect. Interestingly, *With One Voice* was reissued in 1999, including some new hymns and in inclusive language. But no hymn book could keep up with fresh-off-the-press service sheets.

We did experiment with using slide projectors and screens to put the whole service on the wall. We found we were unable to get bright enough images in daylight. Today, Richard's successor is using video projectors and *PowerPoint* to achieve this.

The scan printer enabled us to produce Wedding and Funeral service sheets easily too, so every wedding and funeral had free personalised service sheets. This accompanied an improvement in our bereavement ministry. We offered a cup of tea or coffee to funeral directors and their staff, and a free buffet to mourners after the service. Many families availed themselves of this opportunity, and ladies from the church were always willing to make the buffet and serve it in our coffee bar which had been modernised and improved by some of the church folk.

Incidentally the funeral directors liked the coffee we were serving and so we began selling Traidcraft commodities to them and other people in the community. One of these was the local MP Dennis Turner who lived across the road from us. He was the Chairman of the House of Commons Catering Committee and also Parliamentary Private Secretary to Claire Short, the Minister of Overseas Development. He became excited by Fair Trade because of its support for world-wide social justice, and he was instrumental in the House of Commons in serving Fair

Trade foods, and in Wolverhampton becoming a Fair Trade City.

It was a Black Country tradition for bereaved families to come to an evening service after a funeral. We introduced a monthly Memorial Service which was short and simple and gave us an opportunity to evangelise gently. Up to 200 people attended these monthly services with a small core of church members leading the singing, talking to the guests, and serving them with tea or coffee, where they sat in the Main Worship Hall, as soon as the service ended. One member from each family took a rose from a vase at the back of the hall and placed it in an arrangement on the Holy Table when the name of their deceased person was read out.

Before Christmas we held a Memorial Carol Service in which candles were lit instead of the roses being placed. In the sermon Richard emphasised the commitment of God to us in sending Jesus to be our Saviour. The final hymn was always *Once in Royal David's City* with its last verse:

> Not in that poor lowly stable,
> with the oxen standing by,
> we shall see him, but in heaven,
> set at God's right hand on high;
> there his children gather round
> bright like stars, with glory crowned.

We introduced a monthly non-Eucharistic Family Service which was short and made only one simple Christian point. The children stayed in for the whole service rather than going out to their groups. The intention was that it should be another place where new people could begin. It became well-liked, though may not have been very effective at bringing in new folk. When one of our popular ladies died Richard gathered all the children at his feet and sat amongst them while he told them a story and spoke about death and the Christian's hope of heaven.

All these changes were not without controversy. Long discussions were held which sometimes generated more heat than light. Sometimes in PCC (Parochial Church Council) Richard was forced to rely on a majority vote when he would have preferred unanimity.

Sometimes situations arose for which neither theological college nor curacy had prepared him. For example, early in his ministry as vicar, Richard took the funeral service of an elderly widow who had lived in Bradley all her life. The interment was in a very badly overgrown graveyard a few miles away. A few weeks later one of her children phoned to say that they were concerned about the eldest daughter who had looked after her mother by getting her up, making her breakfast, and putting her to bed every day. Since her mother had died she had continued to go into her mother's house – which was now empty. Every day she still made breakfast for her and carried on as if her mother had not died.

Richard visited the daughter and her husband, and found her not very welcoming or forthcoming. By gentle questioning over several visits Richard found that the daughter had had a son who had died 25 years previously. At five year's old he had become ill. Several times in a week she had taken him to the doctor who grew impatient and told her to go away – but by the end of the week the boy was dead. The daughter's reaction was of rage. She wrote to National newspapers and tried unsuccessfully to get the doctor struck off. 25 years later she was just as angry. Her mother's death had opened old wounds.

It is normal for people in Bradley to visit their loved-ones graves frequently. For some it is a Sunday ritual and the graveyards are covered in fresh flowers all the year round. This lady visited every day. Her father and now her mother were buried there. Visiting was quite an ordeal as the whole graveyard was covered in Japanese knotweed. One day when Richard visited her home she told him that she had found bones on the surface of the grave. At first she threw them away thinking that a dog had brought them but then she found a small jawbone that looked human. Richard was puzzled but she explained that her son had been buried there too and she thought the jawbone belonged to him. She had brought it home with a few other bones that she had found. She also explained that when her son had been buried the hole which had been dug had not been long enough. She and the family had been told to go home and her son would be buried in her absence. Richard began to understand why this poor lady was so disturbed. He asked her what she would like to do about it.

"I'm going to write to the newspapers," she said.

"But what then?" said Richard.

"I want all my son's bones collected and a new funeral," she replied.

In her mind the government, the papers, the medical profession, the church and God were all useless and unsympathetic to her. Richard promised that he would do his best to help her. He said the first step was to find out if these were indeed her son's bones which had somehow come to the surface. She was quite suspicious so he had to promise that whatever he found out he would tell her the truth. He persuaded her to let him take the bones away so that he could find out whether they were human, and the age of the person who had died.

He phoned the local coroner's office and explained the story. Then he took the bones and showed them to a kind lady pathologist who assured him that some of them were from an elderly person – presumably the child's grandfather - and some, including the jawbone, were from a child between 5 and 7 years old. Richard decided that the way forward was to try to stop the child's mother from venting her anger, and give her some peace by laying the whole sad story to rest. He wanted to exhume the grave, sort out the bones and have a graveside service for the boy with a new coffin.

He phoned a senior churchman to run the idea past him. The churchman told him that on no account should he think of an exhumation.

"Tell the lady anything," he said, "but don't countenance an exhumation."

Richard was shocked and decided to ignore this advice. He phoned the office which deals with exhumations in London and eventually got some surprising advice from a sympathetic official. This person asked how hidden the grave was.

"Would it be possible to exhume the grave early in the morning without anyone knowing?"

Richard told him that because of the very tall Japanese knotweed the grave was completely hidden from all directions.

"Then don't apply for an exhumation, Just do it." said the official.

Richard was surprised but contacted the funeral directors. He explained the story and asked them how bones had come to the surface. They contacted the grave-digger and phoned Richard back. The grave-digger had asked a friend to dig the grave for him instead of doing it himself. Apparently when interments are made in old graves, bones are always being uncovered. The usual practice is to gather them together and cover them with earth upon which the new coffin is laid. The friend had not been aware of this. Richard told the funeral directors that he had still not managed to get the agreement of the bereaved lady not to contact the papers. They were concerned about bad publicity. He told them he wanted them to supply a new child's coffin and graveside service free of charge.

By this time the youngest daughter of the original widow was attending prayers each morning in the chapel in the Church

Centre. Richard asked her husband to help him search for the bones which his sister-in-law had thrown away. Together, with one of Richard's sons, they felled about a tennis court in area of the Japanese knotweed and found several bones.

So at 4.00 am a few days later Richard met the funeral directors and the grave-digger at the graveyard. They opened the grave, pulled up the latest coffin and searched for bones. These were placed in a new child's coffin and his grandmother's coffin was returned to the grave and the area tidied up. They all then retired to Richard's Bedford CF camper for a cup of tea. It amused them to see written on a plate at the back of the converted vehicle, *Walker Bodyworks,* the mark of those who had converted it as a camper.

The family had been asked to arrive at 9.00 am and Richard held a graveside service in which the deceased lady, her husband and their little grandson were committed to the earth and to God. They gathered in the home of the troubled lady afterwards for refreshments.

Richard was pleased to find that there was a new peace in the family. Some years later the mother was confirmed in the Church Centre.

Because so many people said, "There ay a church in Bradley," (There isn't a church in Bradley), we held monthly services in different part of the parish on a Sunday morning when the weather was clement. The Brigade band marched ahead behind a wooden cross and the congregation followed. We arrived at an open space or cul-de-sac and held a simple service with a few songs, a Bible reading, a brief message and prayers. Some members took song sheets to those people who came out of their houses, and invited them to join in and offer the names of people for prayer. We also held occasional services in the Primary School and leafleted the area inviting people to join us.

Richard was keen that the church should do evangelism. We booked an evangelist and musician to come for one evening. But before he came some of us went to Nuneaton to see his *performance*. We enjoyed the evening but we thought that there were no people there who were not church-goers. We did not want to use the evening merely to entertain Christians. The whole point was to bring in new people. So we spoke to the evangelist about it. We suggested that there should be a meal and that he would be the after-dinner event. Only church-members who were bringing someone who did not attend any church would be invited, and we would include short challenging but humorous sketches between the evangelist's words and songs. He was keen to support our ideas.

So we had a free (paid for by the church), sit-down cooked meal for 80 people, of whom only 40 were church members. (Some of the church-members who did not invite anyone and who were therefore excluded were not pleased – some of these helped with preparing and serving the meal) After the meal the cabaret began. Richard asked the audience to think what they wanted MOST. He had persuaded 3 members to dress first as babies. These crawled across the floor and sat in a row on the low staging. In a place like Bradley everyone knows everyone else so there was great hilarity. Behind the babies on a huge frieze right across the hall were printed the words, "What do you want MOST?" One baby said, "I want to grow up healthy." Another said, "I want my nappy changed." And the other babies moved a little away from him! The third baby said, "I want someone to love me."

The evangelist spoke and sang some of his songs. Then the babies returned, though now they had become 20 year-olds. Again they said what they wanted most with the last one saying he wanted someone to love him. There was a further contribution from the evangelist saying what Christianity was about. In the final sketch the three actors returned with walking sticks and Zimmer frames. Again they said what they wanted most and the final one said he wanted someone to love him. After this the evangelist sang a final song. Then Richard spoke to the audience challenging them with the question of what they wanted most and saying that only God's love lasted for ever. The people who had been invited to the evening were not total strangers to us. We had been encouraging and speaking to them before, baptising their children, taking funeral services for their loved ones, visiting them, praying for them. Some were neighbours or work-mates of those who had invited them. We felt blessed when 5 of them joined our church. In further evangelism evenings we usually had a meal, always had fun, and built up the fellowship.

One of the things we brought from Guildford was an Agape Supper. This had been introduced to Christ Church by Michael Pain and was a lovely thing. It was a simple meal, held around a large table (many tables put together in a rectangle) and was also a simple Communion Service. It was held on Maundy Thursday in remembrance of Jesus' Last Supper with his disciples before he was arrested and crucified. After the meal, which was part of the service with hymns and prayers, one person (normally a member of the laity) gave an address. Then bread was broken and passed round the group, followed by wine.

The Agape Supper became very popular in St Martin's. Richard wanted to find a large chalice and paten which could be used specifically for this service. One summer we spent a holiday on the Island of Mull off the west coast of Scotland. When we were staying in our camper in Fionnphort, we decided to visit the Isle of Iona and attend worship at the abbey on the Sunday. So we took the ferry and enjoyed the Communion Service. Richard liked the chalices that were used and looked in the shop afterwards to see if similar ones were on sale. We were told to visit the potter whose shop was nearby. But of course on a

Sunday it was closed. So we explored the island and eventually went home.

The next morning Richard suggested that they go back to Iona to see what the potter had to offer. We spent a few minutes on our own in the shop but could find no large chalice. We looked through a door and spotted the potter at his wheel. For a while he did not notice us and we gazed in silence watching the clay rising and falling in his hands. Then he saw us and apologised, asking if he could help us. Richard said that they had been looking for a chalice but were disappointed not to have found one in the shop. The potter said he had felt that something had made him make a chalice today. That was what he was doing.

"I haven't made one for months," he said.

"But we are only here for a few more days," we told him. "The chalice won't be ready will it?"

He explained that he often posted things he had made. So he showed us the design of the chalice and what decoration we could have on it. And we also chose a similar decoration on a pottery paten. The next Maundy Thursday Richard spoke about the lovely new chalice and paten and how they had been provided by the Lord especially for St Martin's Bradley. It was the only time Richard gave the address at an Agape Supper.

When we arrived at St Martin's the church had 3 home-groups. These gradually increased in number. They met in homes and studied the Bible passages used on Sundays and prayed together. We eventually decided to rename the home-groups *cells*. Not like prison cells – more like the cells of a body which could grow in size and divide to grow in number. We had a lot of teaching on cell-church. The cells were intended to be minichurches, studying Scripture, praying, worshipping, doing their own evangelism, engaging in social activities, nurturing new Christians. There were cells for children as well as adults. The intention was to look at the Scriptures we had read on

Sunday morning and ask the question together, "How do I/we apply it to our lives?" Each cell had a host or hosts and 2 leaders, with the intention that, when the cell multiplied, the leaders would separate as well. Some of the cells worked well but the whole project could not truly be called a cell-church. Nonetheless the small groups were important and effective in encouraging discipleship.

At the end of 2002 Richard began to have the feeling that God wanted him to register with Friends Reunited, the website which does exactly what the name suggests. Because even though he had experienced healing there was still tenderness about his secondary school, Richard did not wish to do this. So he didn't. But the feeling grew and, like a kitten lifted by the scruff of its neck, he eventually obeyed.

He registered with the site and looked at the names of people who had been in his year at primary school, university and theological college – but not secondary school. He knew he was not doing what was required and was not surprised that, although he remembered many of the names, no bells rang or lights flashed when he looked at them.

Again, to his shame, he *eventually* obeyed. He popped in the name of the boarding school and looked down the list of names in his year. Now he was surprised. Although he recognised all the names (except that of a girl who had somehow got into the wrong school!), still he did not feel that any were relevant to God's prompting of him. So he looked at the year before the one in which he left. And there he saw the name Roger Durman. How had that happened? Surely Roger was in his year. Why had he left the previous year and how had Richard lost touch with him? Richard couldn't understand it. And so he sent a message to Roger asking him how he was and what he had been doing.

Roger replied immediately saying that he had a lovely wife, a fine son, had done well in his employment and lived in a big house with land in East Lothian, in Scotland. He had just one small black cloud on the horizon. He had recently been diagnosed with an aggressive form of cancer and was not expected to live much longer. How about Richard?

Richard immediately knew that this was what it was about. He replied telling Roger of his teaching, his call to the Anglican ordained ministry, that he was a vicar in a parish between Wolverhampton and Birmingham, and about Celia, Duncan and Justin. He was normally keen not to thrust his faith into the faces of those he was speaking with, but he added at the end of the email, "I am so sorry to hear about your illness. If I were you I would give it to Jesus."

Roger's reply included the line, "I don't understand what you mean. Come and see me."

It was just before Christmas 2002 and we were very busy. But we had one Monday free. And so on Monday 16 December we caught the tram to Birmingham and the first train to Dunbar on a day return. Roger and his wife Penny met us at the station and took us for lunch. We went for a short walk by the sea and returned to their home.

We learned that Roger and Penny had met while putting rings on the legs of wild birds. The birds are caught using nets and, very gently and quickly, a numbered ring is placed on a leg, and the bird released. The information about the bird and the number is stored centrally by the British Trust for Ornithology. If the bird is caught again, or found dead, valuable information can be gained about the bird's movements and age. Both Roger and Penny were very keen and knowledgeable bird-watchers. Penny's particular favourites were swallows which nested in their garden. Penny showed us where they nested and also a hedge that Roger had planted with birds in mind.

Roger was obviously in pain but incredibly brave, thinking of everyone but himself. We had a short conversation and Richard prayed for them – and then it was time to go home on the last train back to Birmingham.

An email awaited us thanking us for going but saying that it had not been long enough. "You clergy must have a break after Christmas, so just let me know when you are coming and I will pay for your flight and arrange for a car to meet you at the airport."

Richard took the situation to the Parochial Church Council.

"I know that my responsibility is in Bradley," he told them, "and so I would like your guidance as to what I should do."

"We can see this is the Lord's work," they said, "Go for as long as you need, and we will look after Bradley."

We caught a plane from Birmingham to Edinburgh early in the morning of 17 February. True to his word Roger arranged for a taxi to collect us and take us to his home in East Linton.

Richard felt that God wanted him to speak with Roger but he was determined that he would not bring up the subject of God. "You have brought us here, now you please make the running," he said to God.

In the afternoon the four of us were in the lounge having a cup of tea when Roger said, "Ladies, Richard and I have some things we wish to discuss, would you please leave us." It was something of a surprise to us, but Celia and Penny dutifully retired.

Richard wondered what he would say next.

"Have you heard of Edward Wilson?" he asked.

"You will have to give me a hint," Richard replied.

"He died with Captain Scott at the South Pole. He was an artist; I have prints of all his pictures He was the expedition doctor. I have been interested in him for over 30 years. Just recently someone gave me a book called *The Faith of Edward Wilson* [6]. I have looked at it but don't understand it. I would like you to explain it to me," said Roger.

Fortunately it was a small book of only 48 pages so Richard was able to read it quickly. As he read he began to wonder if God's purpose in bringing him to Scotland was to get him to read this book. He enjoyed it and learned much from it. He was reminded that he was not the minister. God was the minister to Roger and to him.

He and Roger spent an hour or so together each afternoon and Richard talked with him about the Christian faith. In the end Roger asked for God's forgiveness and said he wanted to receive Jesus as his own Saviour.

Swallows

A prayer for Roger and Penny Durman – 20 February 2003

Lord of the sea and sky and safety,
we thank you for the many bright islands of joy that we have explored.
We thank you for all that we have learned
and all our growing in the Spring and Summer of your love.
We thank you for all your provision and the abundance of our lives.
We thank you for those who have loved us, and those we love,
and those we should have loved more.

Lord there have been times when the cloud and mist have shrouded these islands
and we have become lost, and have forgotten the sun still shining above us.
We have sometimes beaten our wings against the breeze of your gentle purpose,
and made our own directions instead of yours.

We thank you Lord that you have granted us time
and enabled remorse and restitution.
We thank you that the mist has cleared and your way found.

Lord we pray for more islands of warmth and delight,
for exploring and loving and growing and being together.

But we know Lord that winter is approaching;
that dark skies and cold winds will threaten us.
The time for nestling together will soon be over and we will fly
over strange and painful horizons.
Lord we pray that you will fly with us and that there will be
times in our flight
when your warm sun will light our way.

Lord will you guide us?
And if our strength should fail;
our tired wings should cease beating and we fall exhausted to
the ground,
will you come down beside us and pick us up
and take us to that place where we can be revived;
where we can perch and preen with those we love;
where we can be in safety and in joy,
winging the bright skies with you?

When Celia and Richard returned home they tried to get a copy
of *The Faith of Edward Wilson* [6], but it was out of print and
they could not find one. He told the story of God's prompting
and his and Celia's visit to Scotland to his prayer partners, a
Pentecostal and a Baptist minister, at their next monthly
meeting together. They all prayed for Roger and Penny. About
an hour after they had left and gone home Richard received a
phone call from the Baptist Minister,

"A funny thing has happened," he said, "I looked at my
bookshelf and the book, *The Faith of Edward Wilson* [6] was on

it. I've never seen it before so it must be yours. I'll bring it round."

Roger died on 28 April after the swallows had returned. We attended a wonderful service of Thanksgiving and Celebration for his life on 2 May 2003 at Prestonkirk. Penny has become a very good friend.

Corfu May/June 1994

We had not wanted to go to Corfu. The director of the Christian Holiday Company had phoned us, very insistent that we were the right people to lead a holiday. Richard had explained to him that we were very tired from parish ministry; that we had no spare time and that if we did have any it would be for a proper break for us. He phoned again a few days later even more sure that the Lord wanted us to lead a holiday. The person who had recommended us to him is a good friend and so we will not mention his name – but he wasn't flavour of the month for us! The director listened to Richard saying we were not able to help. And then there occurred one of those miracles that we thought we could do without. He asked what time Richard *did* have available. Foolishly Richard replied that the only time we had was one week from Monday to Monday in 6 weeks time. He was confident that this would be too soon and that the start and end date would not fit in with the director's schedule. His reply was that that was exactly the time he was looking for.

Richard said later, "So often I have tried to wriggle out of the Lord's intentions for me. But God picks me up by the scruff of the neck like a cat carrying its kitten. I wriggle and maybe howl but eventually I go along with my Saviour's hopes – and discover that (as Brother Bernard SSF said on my pre-ordination retreat) "God is not a bastard trying to wreck my life". What he intends for me is to bless me, as well, hopefully, as others."

It was a free, expenses paid holiday on Corfu. We stayed in a hotel with 120 other guests. The agreement was that we lead short worship in the morning before breakfast, and a full worship service every evening with a sermon. We also had to make ourselves available to anyone during the day to give Christian counselling. We checked everyone off on our list at Gatwick and were soon in the hotel. We took our responsibilities seriously and ate with different people every meal time. We were surprised how many people wanted to talk to us about spiritual problems. Perhaps they regarded us as safe – and their problems would not reach their home or home church.

We had decided to talk about the book of Ruth in the evenings with its message of God's providence in difficult times.

Sometimes things get really tough for us – the bottom may seem to have dropped out of our world. Maybe we blame God. In the story of Ruth everything goes wrong for Ruth and her mother-in-law. To their credit they continue to bless the Lord. In the end things get better and we can see that God has been working for their good; and not only their own personal welfare but the good of all mankind, as Ruth is revealed as a distant ancestor of Jesus Christ.

We had been promised that people would offer to play musical instruments but in spite of our pleading nobody offered and the worship was hard work. Richard was surprised how many of those who spoke to him were clergy. It was not till the end of the week that someone told us that the previous week had been for clergy only and that they had been offered a discount on a second week.

The sun shone. It was a beautiful environment. Everyone was enjoying themselves but we felt oppressed. Celia became unwell. We prayed about it but did not feel able to share the problems with anyone there.

Before the worship on the Friday evening someone came to us and said that there *were* folk who played musical instruments and had them with them! They were feeling that they had let us down. Would we like them to play? So for the first time the worship was good that evening and we could let them lead. On the Sunday morning it was Holy Communion, a truly joyful occasion with Christians of many denominations. It felt as if something good had happened apart from the contribution of the musicians – as if the Lord had done some great work.

After the service a couple came to us and asked if we would like to come back to their self-catering flat and have a cup of coffee. He was a clergyman. His wife had been suffering from depression for many years. They had tried all kinds of therapy and prayer to no avail. Eventually she had lost her faith. The world had become black. She said that during the previous week the darkness had begun to lift and that during our week it had continued and that she felt now that there was light at the end of the tunnel, and that God really loved her. Her husband said that he knew we had had a difficult week and that it might encourage us to hear their story.

And then the Lord did a wonderful thing. It was time for us to go back to the hotel for lunch. We prayed together, thanking God for his wonderful love, and asking him to continue his work of healing in all our lives. We rose to go. Richard shook hands with the husband and then turned to his wife. She put her hand out to him but instead of taking it Richard said, "That is the wrong hand. It is the other one that the Lord wants to bless." Richard did not understand what he was saying.

She looked shocked. "Do you know?" she asked. Richard said that he felt that he was out of his depth. She peeled back the long sleeve of her blouse on her left arm. In horrid scars it said, "I HATE ME". The large letters had been scribed with a Stanley knife in an attempt at suicide a few years before.

We still did not understand, but believed that in some way the Lord had used us to help and rescue this lady, and in doing so had confirmed his wonderful love for us, and shown in a practical modern way the message of Ruth.

On the last evening it was the custom to have worship with testimonies, to which anyone could contribute, of what the Lord had done or been saying to them during the week. There were various heart-warming anecdotes and many thanks to God for his generosity and his wonderful creation. Then the clergyman's wife rose and told her story of how she had known the depths of depression and how the Lord had rescued her and confirmed it with his wonderful words through Richard. Great was the rejoicing.

We have visited the couple in their home in England and continued to keep in touch. It has been thrilling to know that she has continued in the faith, knowing the Lord's love.

Walkers on legs

Even before we were married we were both walkers. Celia had walked over the South Downs with her parents and friends. She had holidayed in the Lake District with her father. Richard had walked with family and friends in Yorkshire, the Lake District and Scotland. When we were at Keele University we walked together in the North Staffordshire countryside and also through the Potteries' towns. We often walked along deserted railway tracks. Once we explored a railway line which we thought was not used on Sundays. We walked through a dark tunnel. As we emerged into the sunshine a steam engine pulling a goods train followed us.

We are members of the Ramblers' Association and give money and time to help the wonderful network of footpaths in Britain to be in good order. Once we carried our petrol mower across several fields to help open up a public footpath which had become overgrown. We don't usually walk in large groups but prefer our own company, and possibly that of one or two friends. We look out for the natural world, and for old or interesting buildings or archaeology. We prefer to be able to change our minds, to stop or continue as we wish.

During our lifetime, long-distance footpaths have been designated. The idea of walking in the company of loads of other people and stopping overnight in crowded bunkhouses does not appeal, but the idea of walking a long way is attractive. Once we used youth hostels in the Lake District. It was in term time so we thought they would not be crowded. In fact one was a nightmare of unsupervised and poorly behaved schoolchildren. Other times we have carried a tent and stayed in wild places which we have found much more enjoyable.

We back-packed with our sons in Snowdonia when they were quite small, and the Lake District when they were teenagers.

Walk to the Coast

In May 1992 we walked from Bradley in the West Midlands to Tywyn in West Wales. Over the previous winter we did many training walks in the conurbation and through the countryside. Sometimes we carried a couple of house bricks in our rucksacks to simulate the load we would be taking.

We hoped to keep off roads and use tracks and paths. We bought all the 1:25,000 Ordnance Survey maps to the west of Wolverhampton, and planned a route. We wrote to various rural sub-post offices and obtained advice about where we could bed-and-breakfast. This was before we had use of the Internet.
We set off at eight o'clock on the May Bank Holiday morning. Walking beside the Bradley Arm canal we were soon at the mainline canal between Birmingham and Wolverhampton. The way to Wolverhampton was lined with derelict buildings and the former site of the Bilston Steelworks. We carried no camping equipment – mainly clothes, water, a little food and a shiny brass paraffin stove – but the old rucksacks we were using weighed heavily on our shoulders. After 5 miles we were pleased to reach the top lock of the Wolverhampton flight and stopped for a cup of coffee, cooked on our paraffin stove.
We had walked this way several times while training over the winter. The locks had been emptied and cleaned and were now looking spick and span. A family were playing by the canal, splashing a child in a small rubber dinghy in the warm sunshine. We reached the Staffordshire and Worcester Canal at the bottom of the flight and crossed over the bridge to the tow path on the other side.

As we walked we noticed and made a list of the wild plants, birds and animals we saw: reed buntings, a whitethroat singing, a family of moorhens, coots, various different species of butterfly, ragwort, white campion, cranesbill, horsetails.

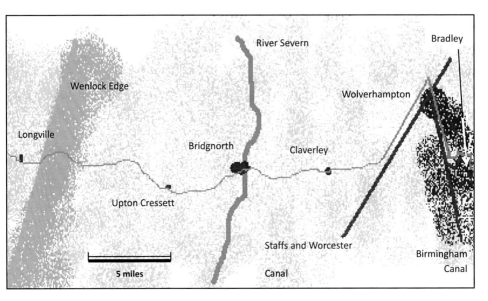

River Severn

Bradley

Wenlock Edge

Wolverhampton

Longville

Bridgnorth

Claverley

Upton Cressett

Staffs and Worcester

Birmingham
Canal

5 miles

Canal

Dunstall Park racecourse was on the other side of the canal as we headed south west. The weather became quite hot as we passed a few locks and under several bridges. We stopped at Mop's Farm Bridge and found a shady spot to have lunch. Then we continued south-west along a track past farms and villages, resting occasionally to enjoy the view, until we arrived in the evening at Claverley. We ate in the Plough Inn and stayed overnight with Mrs Elcock in her bungalow up the High Street.

The following morning after breakfast we continued through the lanes and along footpaths. Some of these had entirely disappeared on the ground but we struggled on, finding broken stiles indicating that we were on the right route. Eventually we found our way blocked by an industrial estate with no sign of the footpath which the map indicated continuing through it. We were forced on to the main road and walked beside it down the hill into Bridgnorth. Immediately after the bridge across the River Severn we used the cliff railway to ascend to High Town and had lunch in a café at the top overlooking the panorama.

We walked through the town and emerged in undulating countryside. By small lanes and field paths we arrived at a delightful valley in which we found a Norman Church next to an Elizabethan manor house. This was called Upton Cressett after a member of the Upton family married a member of the Cressett family in the 14th century. The village was in decline even in the 14th century and was deserted some time later. The church had been closed for worship in 1959. There was a notice saying where we could obtain the key to let us in. Instead, we continued our walk through the churchyard as we had a long way to go.

After only half a mile on a footpath we came to a lane at New House Farm. The path opposite was blocked so we reluctantly headed north down the lane to Monkhampton. We had planned our route to be almost entirely on footpaths so it was disappointing to be walking along the fairly busy B4368. At Weston we turned right to Brockton and found what had been a public footpath by the school. It was not waymarked, nor were the stiles in good order, but we ploughed on regardless, even through a growing crop. When we were almost in sight of our destination the bridleway passed through a wood. Sadly the wood had been felled and tree-trunks were lying on top of one another like Spillikins. It took us a long time to negotiate them. Eventually we emerged on Wenlock Edge, walked down the hill, and arrived at 9.00 pm at the Longville Arms where we had arranged to stay the night.

Because we had a long way to go the next day we told Mrs Egan, the landlady, that we wished to leave at 6.00 am the following morning. She kindly made us some sandwiches filled with slabs of beef instead of a cooked breakfast. We left on a pleasant sunny morning. Because we thought the paths might again be in poor order we stayed on the road, first to Wall-under-Heywood then north through Stoneacton until we saw a bridleway on our left. This was a lovely path across open grassland with rocks and sheep.

A lovely path across open grassland with rocks and sheep

We stopped to eat our beef sandwiches and watched a fox crossing the track. Then we continued down the hill south of Caer Caradoc and into Church Stretton. We bought some pasties and soft drinks for lunch and made our way up Carding Mill Valley, continuing over the Long Mynd. It was quite hot walking over the moorland. We descended the western edge of the Mynd and ate our lunch near Manor Farm. Because of a blocked path we decided to leave our planned route and walked on a farm track to Adstone and then on a quiet road to Wentnor where we stopped for a cool drink at The Crown. The very long walk of the day before, the blocked and overgrown paths – at one point we had put on overtrousers to wade through nettles – the heat, and the uncomfortable rucksacks were beginning to get us down. In the pub we decided to call a taxi which took us 10 miles to Blue Barn, half a mile north of Church Stoke.

We walked up a lane to The Brynkin where we rejoined our intended route. We crossed the River Camlad by a footbridge and went on the minor road to Rhiston. We had expected to have a quick and quiet walk by footpaths across fields to Little Brompton Farm where we had booked dinner, bed and breakfast. In the event the paths were non-existent and we had to guess where they had been. We kept records of all the places where we encountered difficulties with paths and on our return informed the local authorities responsible for their maintenance. We did not suppose much action would be taken. We arrived at our accommodation just in time for dinner, feeling somehow guilty about having taken the taxi but glad that we had as we would not have got to the farm by dark.

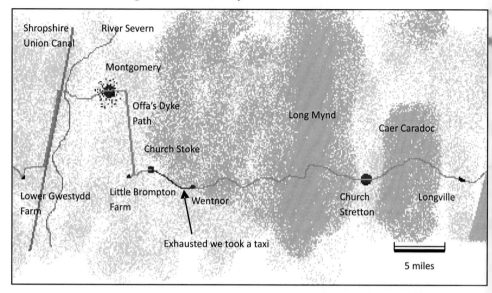

The next day had been intended as a much shorter walk through farmland. After our experiences in the previous two days we decided to abandon the direct route and go first north-west to Montgomery along Offa's Dyke Path and then south-west along the Shropshire Union Canal. We hoped both of these would be easier walking. They were easier though there are many stiles along Offa's Dyke Path which were quite tiring to negotiate.

We sat in the town square in Montgomery, wrote a few postcards, and bought a quiche, and fruit and nut slice, for lunch. Then we walked up to the castle and had a good view of the Milk Race as the Tour of Britain cycle race was called. After the cyclists came estate cars, and vans carrying cycles and large notices saying RACE CONTROL, TRAFFIC CONTROL. The final one had some brushes peering out of the roof and a sign saying BROOM CONTROL. We then continued on the road over the River Severn and joined the canal at Trwstllewelyn.

Soon after joining the towpath we passed a collection of animals including pot-bellied pigs and llamas as well as exotic birds. Near these alien species were yellow flag irises and water crowsfoot. A road bridge had been built low across the canal at one point showing that there was no intention of re-opening the canal to boats.

The past few days had been very hot. Today in the afternoon it became sultry and after the clouds had built for a while the heavens opened. There was first a warning shower from which we sheltered under Brynderwen Bridge. Sensible people would have taken the hint and retreated indoors, but we had to get to our accommodation. We left the canal at Aberbechan and with only 2 miles to go set off up the lane. We were dry for over a mile but then an enormous thunderstorm poured its rain on us. We had moderately efficient wet-weather gear but this was useless in the cataclysm. There was no shelter. The lane became a torrent so that water was flowing over our boots. We arrived at Lower Gwestydd Farm – a lovely black and white house – and were welcomed by Mrs Jarman, very sympathetic but also apologetic because the storm had caused a power cut. She insisted on us bathing in their family bathroom and, most kindly, dried our things by their Rayburn which also cooked our evening meal, which we enjoyed by candlelight.

There was still some light rain in the morning. We took out the newspapers that we had put in our sodden boots and set off about 9.15. We had originally planned this walk, with maps spread out right across our lounge carpet, to be almost entirely on footpaths. Because of the dilapidated or overgrown state of so many in the past days we used lanes and small roads this morning.

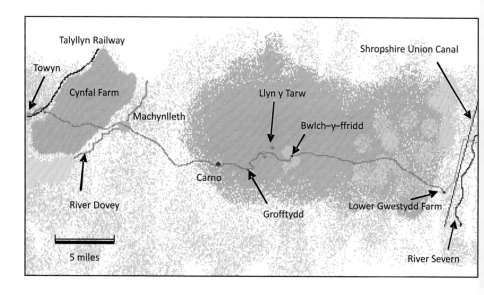

The weather cleared up and soon we were walking down the hill into Bwlch–y–ffridd. We asked a couple in their garden if there was a shop where we could buy some things for lunch. They laughed and said that the nearest shop was in Newtown. After hearing where we had come from and where we were headed they invited us in and gave us a light lunch. Soon we were on our way again up the road to Bwlch–cae-haidd. There we struck off across the mountains, using the magnetic compass to keep the direction correct. Some wheatears flew ahead of us. We had a cup of tea by the lake Llyn y Tarw where we saw black-headed gulls nesting on the two islands. Failing to find the bridleway between the two lakes Llyn Mawr and Llyn Du, we eventually descended the steep hillside to Pantegesail and via a track and road to Grofftydd where we were welcomed by Mrs Pru Lewis. She fed us a lovely meal including home-made soup and salad. It was a glorious evening. We sat and looked at the map, planning the next day's walk, and watched a spotted flycatcher catching its supper from the fence opposite.

131

We left at 8.00 am and walked on the road reaching Carno as rain began heavily. We bought some scotch eggs and flapjacks for lunch. As we set off across the hill towards Trannon the sun came out and we were able to take our raingear off. It was beautiful and remote countryside. A snipe flew off with its characteristic zigzag flight. Then we descended to the road near Maes-ymdrisiol and headed south. We turned right and continued west, stopping at some lovely waterfalls to eat lunch. Eventually the road became Glyndwr's Way which we followed all the way to Machynlleth.

On Glyndwr's Way we enjoyed splendid mountain views. At Cefnwyrygu we spoke to a farmer who had lived there for 70 years. Some of the way was rough and steep and we began to be quite tired but, in contrast to some of the previous paths, it was well way-marked. We entered Machynlleth past the golf course and soon found our accommodation with Mrs Vince who gave us another good meal. After a long hot bath we were soon asleep.

We left after breakfast and crossed the quiet town on the Sunday morning. We set off north and crossed the River Dovey.

The bridge across the Dovey

Turning left we walked along the main A493 for 3 miles to Cwrt. Then we took a byway open to all traffic but very quiet on the right hand side for just over a mile. We branched off to the right on a steep track over the mountains. As we reached a high point we could see the sea in the distance ahead of us. As everywhere Celia made a list of the wildlife we saw. Here it was heather, ling, bilberries, cotton grass and lousewort. There were ravens and goldfinches in the air and a hare bounding across the open terrain.

It wasn't long before we descended to the Talyllyn Railway and Cynfal farm where Mrs Evans and her two children welcomed us.

The next morning there was no hurry. The weather was wet and we only had about 4 miles to reach the sea. We spent 15 minutes on the beach, ate an ice cream, and went to the Railway Station where we caught a train to Dovey Junction and another to Wolverhampton and home.

South-west Coast Path

On Monday 2 August 1999 we took the train from Birmingham to Penzance, a journey most of which we had made several times with our Church Lads' and Church Girls' Brigade Company on our way to *camp* in St Ives. We put on our rucksacks and alighted in slight drizzle. We bought 2 pasties and immediately set off back the way we had come, walking between the railway and the sea.

After a short while we left the railway and continued along the coast through Marazion. St Michael's Mount stood mysterious and magnificent on our right. Only a short distance later we put up the tent in a corner of a field, cooked a meal, and went to bed. The tent was modern, small and quite light.

The following morning was sunny. We ate some breakfast, packed up our things into the rucksacks and set off again along the South-West Coast Path. These were new rucksacks and much more comfortable than the ones we had carried on our walk across Wales. We were soon going up and down over hills. We found it quite tiring and realised we were not going to complete large distances each day. We told each other that we were not trying to prove anything to anyone, so we scrapped our itinerary with its estimates of how far we would cover each day in order to get to Brixham by the time the Brigade arrived on 21 August. We were each carrying a one litre water bottle which needed replenishing quite frequently. Although we journeyed into what seemed quite wild places we were never very far from habitation. Some houses were right on the cliff top and we chose one behind Bessy's Cove to ask for water. The inhabitants were sunbathing on loungers and seemed almost jealous of us being able to walk along the path so freely. Richard offered to swap with them but they didn't take up his offer. They did however fill up our bottles.

We ate our pasties in a shady niche in the rocks near Hoe Point, because it was hot in the sun, and cooked a cup of tea on our little stove. This was new also. Our paraffin stove had been quite heavy and so we had bought a little gas Trangia – very neat, quick to operate, efficient and light. Then up and down again until we came to Praa Sands where we ate some chips in the café, and then walked along the beach among the holiday-makers. We managed to collect some more water from stationary holiday-makers further on, who told us that we would avoid blisters if we urinated in our boots – advice we were careful not to take! As we ascended Rinsey Head a thick sea mist rolled in and it became cool and damp. The chimney of an old tin mine passed us in the gloom. Then the mist cleared and we pitched our tent on Tremearne Cliff with splendid views over the sea.

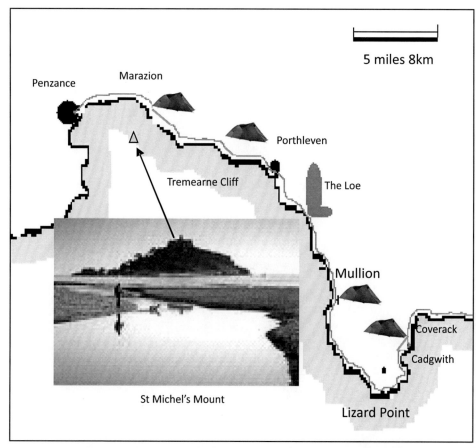

Penzance
Marazion
Porthleven
Tremearne Cliff
The Loe
Mullion
Coverack
Cadgwith
St Michel's Mount
Lizard Point

5 miles 8km

Richard went out about midnight to check the tent and enjoyed the stars and the lights to the west. But we heard it begin to rain about 6.30 am and we made an error. We got up! Packing the rucksacks we managed to get things a bit wet as with this tent we could not leave the fly sheet erected while we packed up the inner tent. We got out of the rain in a bus shelter but then continued into Porthleven. Having walked beside the harbour and seen the rain drops splattering on the water between the moored boats, there before us was a most inviting notice which spoke of a Big Breakfast. We failed to resist the temptation and a few moments later were taking off our outside wet things in a little café. We spent a couple of hours there and enjoyed a very big breakfast, and dried off quite well.

Just before we were in danger of having to partake of a Big Lunch the rain stopped and the sun came out. Steam was rising from the road as we headed south-east after walking round the other side of the harbour. It was quite hot as we descended towards Loe Bar. A lad who had sensibly stayed in his tent while it was raining was just striking camp as we overtook him and left the Loe freshwater lake on our left. The lad passed us as we had a rest and a cup of coffee a kilometre further on. We didn't see him again.

We felt we didn't have time or energy to go down the steep cliffs of the Dollar Cove so we missed the opportunity to look for some of the gold coins supposedly lost there in a shipwreck in the 18th century. We did however walk across the beach at Church Cove to admire the little church strangely separated from its tower. Just a short distance further on we came to Poldhu Cove. This is the location of Guglielmo Marconi's transmitter for the first transatlantic radio message on

December 12, 1901 to a receiving station on Signal Hill, St. John's, Newfoundland. The 27 year-old Marconi spent vast amounts of his father's money on an experiment which all the scientists of his day agreed was impossible, because they had not then discovered the ionosphere. He succeeded at the first attempt and later received the Nobel Prize for Physics. We made good progress until we climbed the steep side of Mullion Cove and collapsed on the cliff-top where we could see the National Trust harbour. We decided that was far enough for that day.

The National Trust Harbour at Mullion Cove

In the morning we dried out our wet things in the sunshine. As we travelled down the west side of the Lizard Peninsula we found the terrain much flatter, open moorland. It was easier going and we made good progress. We saw soay sheep and many wild flowers. There were very few people about though we met the occasional south-west coast path walker going the opposite way. Two young men from the Netherlands had come from the beginning of the path on the shore of Poole Harbour and were intending to walk the whole 630 miles via Lands End to Minehead.

Few people there were until we came to Kynance Cove. We thought the nearby car park as well as the beautiful location and sunny weather might have attracted the hundreds of people clustered on the beach. We descended to join them and bought a Cornish ice-cream and cup of tea.

When we came to the Lizard Point we joined hundreds more people watching a helicopter and RNLI Lifeboat giving a demonstration of a rescue. At Housel Bay Richard waited with the rucksacks while Celia went to Lizard to buy some provisions. Then we walked on and found ourselves a place to camp on the cliffs at Landewednack, a former Caravan Club site which is now owned by the National Trust. From the cliff top we watched men and women from Cadgwith in skiffs training for racing.

Cadgwith

In the morning we set off again but it soon began to rain. This necessitated another big breakfast in Cadgwith, a tiny working fishing village in a cove, with thatched cottages. We noticed the boathouse where we presumed the skiffs had come from. The rain stopped and we set off again up the steep path to over 60 metres. Over our whole walk we must have ascended thousands of feet (and lots of metres!).

We continued east with great views over the rocks and sea. There were always yachts near in and further offshore and we began to wonder about the possibility of us sailing along this coast. We had a brief rest at Kennack Sands with a cup of tea and a doughnut. At the lovely valley above Downas Cove we met a lone walker from Sheffield who told us he was a fan of the Lizard. Our camping place for the night was on top of Chynhalls Cliff overlooking Chynhalls Point with its Iron Age ramparts showing that people have been living in this area for a long time.

The tiny harbour at Coverack

The next day we were soon at Coverack with its tiny harbour crammed with boats. We enjoyed an ice cream while watching all the buzz of holidaymakers, and locals preparing for the regatta that afternoon. We sent some clotted cream from Roskilly's Farm Shop to various friends and relatives. At a cottage a little further on we were asked by a Spaniard and

Ukrainian to take a photo of them. The path beyond Coverack at first ascended to 40 metres and then went down beside the rocky beach. We ate lunch here on the beach with a view of Chynhalls Point and Coverack. It was very hot.

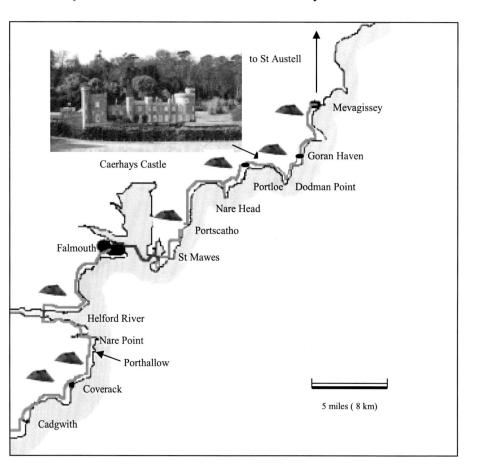

At this point we were a little uncertain of the way. We passed Dean's Quarry which mines Gabbro (sometimes unhelpfully called Black Granite), climbed a steep valley to Rosenithon and walked along a lane up to 75 metres. Somehow we found ourselves at Roskilly's Farm where we had some apple juice and more ice cream – this time blackberry flavoured. We came out at the sea again and climbed up to an old quarry cliff ledge where we pitched the tent. Several people with dogs passed, including a father and son from Wales, and an English/French couple who allowed us to accompany them to their cottage and gave us some water.

Out to sea we watched a large cruise liner pass heading east. Then the night became wet and windy as we slept in our little tent.

The rain had stopped so we were away early in the morning, past the cottage where we had obtained water, and on through the lanes until we joined the coast again at Porthallow. Here we had coffee and scones at the Taranaki Tea Gardens. We were not sure if we smelt bad, but the kind owner Dorothy Pelling offered us showers which we accepted. We had decided to catch the bus to Helford and so we went out to the bus stop and waited a long time for the rare bus. It came, fairly well on time. We put out a hand to stop it, bent down to pick up our rucksacks, and it drove off again. We were a little miffed, but put on brave faces with the rucksacks, and headed off along the coast path.

After Porthallow the path took us along the cliff top again past Nare Point where there were good views all round including the next great obstacle: the Helford River. We were soon down in Gillan and its neighbour Flushing. The path goes right round Gillan Creek, a journey of over 2 miles, but we came upon a young boy doing not very much in a motor boat. We asked if he would like to take us across the creek which he was keen to do. After he had checked with his grandparents in a nearby house he took us across and we gave him a small amount of money. We walked up on to Dennis Head and then returned to the SW Coastpath westwards through the woods along the south bank of the Helford River to Helford.

Here we took the official ferry to the north side. We walked up the lane and for the first time on this expedition failed to find a suitable place to camp. Eventually we decided upon a rough field in which a barn was being converted into a house. Nobody was about so we pitched our tent. Then we returned to the Ferry Boat Inn, busy with a regatta fun day. We ate slightly cardboard-tasting veggie burgers followed by apple and banoffi pies at the barbecue.

The next day we were up early and set off without breakfast, before the builders arrived, and caught a bus to Falmouth. We located a laundrette and arranged for the woman there to look after our things, leaving us free to eat a big breakfast on the pier and discover ferry times. After collecting the washing, we caught the 11.15 am ferry to St Mawes and then a smaller boat to Place. It was a hot day again and we had forgotten to fill up our water containers so we asked at a National Trust cottage where friendly holidaymakers obliged. We toiled up the hill, passing the white lighthouse on St Anthony's Head, and admiring Atlantic grey seals far below as we travelled to Zone Point.

After heading north up and down along the cliffs and down to near sea level, we camped justbefore Porthscatho. We thought it was about to rain so we pitched the tent hurriedly on a rough piece of reedy ground by the shore. There was a sign nearby pointing to farm camping further away. In the evening we explored Porthscatho and walked up to Gerrans before retiring to our little tent.

In the morning we were visited by an angry farmer, complaining that we were camping by the shore free of charge. It was not our finest camping moment so we gave him £5 to soothe his temper and set off again in warm sunshine.

On the beach near Porthcurnick we spied an ice cream booth from a long distance away. We approached it in anticipation but noticed when close that it was advertising Nestlé ice cream. We have boycotted Nestlé products since learning of the way they distribute baby-milk powder free of charge to nursing mothers in Africa. The firm were criticised for making the mothers, who did not have the wherewithal to sterilise bottles, dependent on the milk substitute, thereby causing the deaths of thousands of babies.

"Do you have any other make of ice-cream than Nestlé?" we asked the girl in the booth.

"No, I'm sorry I don't." she replied.

We explained why, sadly, we could not buy it from her, and walked on un-ice-creamed.

After making good progress fairly level near the beach we climbed up to the top of Nare Head, a very warm 100 metres high. Then we walked up and down smaller hills until we reached Manare Point where we stopped for the night near a chicken farm.

The next day was 11 August 1999. It was the day when a total solar eclipse was supposed to be visible in south-west England. This was the reason why we had chosen to go for a long walk in Cornwall at this time. We walked down to Portloe and settled with others on Jacka Point, a headland between the village and the sea. Portloe is a pretty village which has avoided much development. The original lifeboat station quite high on the hill is now a church. Launching the boat was a difficult operation which required her to be hauled down the hill, then swivelled around and let down the steep slope onto the beach. Once, during a practice session, she ran out of control and crashed into a shop. A new lifeboat house was then built up against the cliff on the shoreline. In fact in the whole 17 years that Portloe had a lifeboat, it was not once able to make a rescue because whenever there was a storm the harbour was practically impossible to get out of.

Today the village was going to get dark in the day time. There were many eclipse watchers, on the cliffs, balconies and other vantage points. They were in festive mood and some waved flags and sang *Land of Hope and Glory*. The snag was that, after several sunny days, it was cloudy. Nonetheless lots of people turned out and the sky began to get dark and the air cold. We put on more clothes. The gulls seemed quite upset – calling wildly.

In a total eclipse of the Sun a circular shadow of the Moon is thrown on the Earth. As it got dark the gulls went quiet. When we were experiencing the greatest darkness it was not completely dark because miles away we could see light at the edge of the shadow. Slowly the shadow passed overhead and then it gradually got light again. At one point the clouds broke a little and we could see that the sun's disc was not complete – but the view was not great.

After the eclipse we set off again and bought two pasties which we ate, still warm, at Hartriza Point. There was much up and down until we reached West Portholland where we saw first, two walkers in kilts, then a lone man who looked like David Bellamy, and finally a party of people heading west, eager to tell us about the eclipse they had seen. In East Portholland we had tea and coffee and walnut cake from the post office, and talked with a couple from the Methodist Church who worked with pensioners and also enjoyed walking.

Soon we passed Caerhays Castle. The original castle was owned by the Trevanion family from 1390. They provided Sheriff's of Cornwall for several monarchs in the 16th century, as well as a Naval Commander and a parliamentarian. But William Trevanion, who served in parliament for the borough of Tregony, and died in 1767 without children, left the male line of this family extinct. He was succeeded by Mr John Bettesworth, his sister's son. *His* son John Bettesworth Trevanion inherited it in 1801 at the age of 21. He employed the architect John Nash to build the present mansion which was completed in 1808. That building work combined with gambling bankrupted the family who fled to Bruges in 1840 leaving the castle to their creditors. It was left for 13 years and eventually bought – almost derelict – by a mine owner, Michael Williams, in 1853. He restored it. The Williams family, who have stocked the gardens with imported rhododendrons, camellias and magnolias, still live in the property. We passed by the castle and camped on Greeb Point.

Climbing Dodman Point

Please do not think that this was a flat cliff-top walk. Today as we came out of our tent we looked up Dodman Point which was our next target. At 120 metres (400 feet) it was the highest point on our walk. After accepting some water from an elderly couple in a cottage by Hemmick Beach, we struggled up and made an early cup of coffee on our little gas stove, seated at the foot of a large granite cross placed there in 1896 by the Reverend George Martin, Rector of nearby St Michael, Caerhays.

The text says:

IN THE SURE HOPE OF THE
SECOND COMING
OF THE LORD JESUS CHRIST
AND FOR THE
ENCOURAGEMENT OF THOSE
WHO STRIVE TO SERVE HIM
THIS CROSS IS ERECTED 1896.

The cross is intended therefore neither as an aid to shipping nor a memorial. It is more a spiritual signpost.

We descended to Goran Haven and found some plaice and chips which we ate in the shade by the path. We explored the main street and bought bread and baked beans to go with the pasties we had bought in East Portholland. Then we walked on to Pabyer Point and camped on the cliffs. In the evening we walked into Portmellon and admired a square-rigged sailing ship anchored in the bay.

The following day we made unexpected progress. We walked in to Mevagissey and, because we had run out of money, searched for an ATM to obtain some more. We asked in the post office where we might find one and were told that the nearest was in St Austell. The post-master was about to go there and offered us a lift. But then he decided not to go so we caught a bus.

After obtaining some cash, we went off to the railway station. We needed to be in Brixham by Saturday 21 August to meet the Brigade. Today was Friday 13 August so we needed to cover a lot of ground quickly. We caught an express train to Totnes and then a bus to Kingsbridge where we enquired of the Tourist Information Office and found a very nice bed and breakfast in a bungalow overlooking the estuary. So we had moved swiftly from Cornwall to Devon. After a cooked breakfast we caught an early ferry down the river to Salcombe.

The view from the window of the bungalow in Kingsbridge

In Salcombe we found the land base of the Island Cruising Club. They also have a ship, the Egremont, a converted Mersey ferry, which is used as a base for sailing courses and holidays. We went into a large room full of ancient (and not so ancient) mariners and asked at reception what we had to do to charter a yacht. We were told that most yacht charterers require an RYA Dayskipper Theory and Practical qualification as a minimum. They said they were themselves a school for RYA qualifications and there were other schools all over the country. We resolved to research this more when we got home. (In fact we started the theory course online almost immediately we returned home, and when we had finished that, took the practical examination in Plymouth the following June.)

We caught the ferry across the estuary to East Portlemouth and resumed our walk. Earlier it had been quite misty but now the sun blazed down and it became hot. We came upon the Gara Hotel, converted from a row of cottages, high on the cliffs. We sat on the terrace and were served an ice cream. Then we were off again to Prawle Point where Richard was not feeling well but the Coast watch volunteers refused us the use of their toilet.

That night we camped on Langerstone Point. Celia was interested in the schists with glacial deposits above the raised beach and a Pleistocene cliff line.

It was very windy overnight but in the morning Richard felt better. We made our way onward, past more glacial deposits. In her geological mode Celia pointed out the stacks at Great Mattiscombe Sand. We passed Start Point with its lighthouse, and then went down to Hallsands, Beesands and Torcross. We learned the story of the fishing village of Hallsands that had been built below the cliffs. It developed to 39 houses in the 18th and 19th centuries, protected by its pebble beach. But in 1890, the Admiralty decided that the naval dockyard at Keyham near Plymouth should be expanded. A vast amount of shingle was required. A firm was awarded a contract to dredge the pebbles from the sea between Beesands and Hallsands. The villagers protested and some slight compensation was paid. They were assured that the sea would soon replenish any pebbles that were taken. When the beach did fall, some new sea walls were built

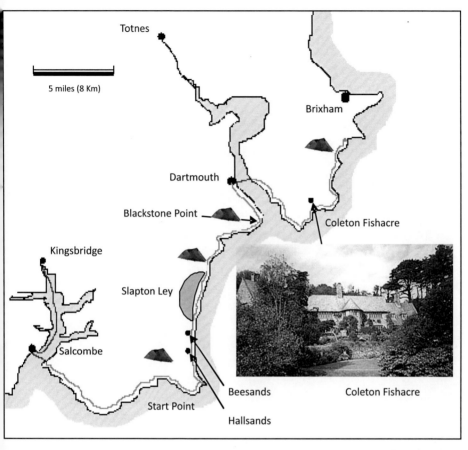

Coleton Fishacre

but eventually in a great storm on 26 January 1917 Hallsands was demolished by the waves. Fortunately no-one was killed.

One family made homeless was that of Mrs Eliza Trout, a fisherman's widow, and her four daughters, Patience, Ella, Clara and Edith. The Trouts used some compensation money and a bank loan to build a new home for themselves, which they planned to make into a guest house that they called Prospect House. Patience and Ella did much of the work themselves, digging the foundations, carrying shingle and boulders from the beach to make concrete blocks, and installing a water supply

149

from a source up the valley. As fisherwomen, they were not afraid of hard work! The completed guest house was so successful that the Trout sisters extended the building, and by 1933 it was a hotel catering for up to 70 guests. The hotel's reputation grew and grew, and affluent guests would return year after year. The sisters continued to fish, and treated their guests to fresh fish, crab and lobster dinners.

We had some chocolate cake and a cup of tea at Trout's, served by a girl from Birmingham.

The Hallsands demolition was during the First World War. Another and altogether greater tragedy occurred during the Second World War further along at Slapton Sands. Our first intimation of this was a Sherman tank just beyond Torcross. It commemorates the tragic farce of Exercise Tiger in December 1943 when American troops were preparing for the D-Day landings. Slapton Sands was chosen for its similarity to Utah beach (also gravel and not sand!) The result was a farcical tragedy in which 946 Americans were killed by a combination of fire from German E-boats, incorrect use of life-vests, and firing on the beach by their own side with the soldiers going over marker lines intended to keep them safe. The number dying in the practice was much higher than those killed in the actual landing on D-Day.

We plodded along the gravel bar which is Slapton Sands with the freshwater Slapton Ley on our left. At the Northern end we came to a notice advertising a Caravan and Camping Club site where we spent the night. We decided to give ourselves a day off the next day and spent it exploring the nearby Slapton Ley Nature Reserve. In the campsite we saw some rabbits and on the road a weasel, which may not have been good news for the rabbits. In the evening we treated ourselves to a meal at the Ship Inn: salmon and asparagus sauce with seasonal vegetables with an Australian wine, followed by apple pie for one and treacle tart for the other.

In the morning it was raining. This time we did not make a mistake. We got up only to have a warm shower and bought a paper at the shop. The rain stopped after lunch and we went to Dartmouth on the bus. It was a white-knuckle ride in the front seat of a double-decker. After exploring the quay and looking at the boats we bought some courgettes and pasta. Then we had a cream tea before returning to the tent on another bus.

Walking the following day was not especially pleasant. Local landowners had clearly won the battle to keep the path away from the coast. We sheltered from a shower on Blackpool Sands so we had another big breakfast there. We were beginning to get used to them! The sun came out and we stopped in a bus shelter for a drink of water. While we were sitting there, a shower which we had not seen coming, deluged the shelter. At the end of the day we pitched our tent on Blackstone Point at the mouth of the River Dart.

Camping on Blackstone Point

In the night Celia was unwell with an upset stomach. The tent was not the best place to be so in the morning we walked to Dartmouth Castle. Richard left Celia sitting on a shady seat and watching the boats. One she saw was Inventure, a trimaran with

151

Walker Wingsails (vertical aerofoils), being tested. Richard went into Dartmouth and found first a guest house where the landlady was happy for Celia to go to bed. He then found a launderette and eventually managed to persuade a machine to wash and dry some clothes. While it was working Richard sat on a seat overlooking the Dart and chatted to a lady from Dorchester who happened to know his cousin Avril through their church.

The following day Celia pronounced herself better and able to continue, so, after haddock for breakfast, we took the nearby vehicle ferry across to Kingswear. It was a strange flat vessel propelled by a tug which pulled and pushed it alongside itself. We resumed following the SW Coast path overlooking the river with its castle and then the sea. We passed a plaque in memoriam of Lt Col. H Jones of the Parachute Regiment who received a posthumous VC after the Falklands War.

We continued on the cliff top and admired Shetland Ponies introduced by the National Trust to keep the grassland in good shape.

In the early 1920s Sir Rupert and Lady Dorothy D'Oyly Carte, of Gilbert and Sullivan opera fame, were sailing their yacht from Brixham to Dartmouth when they noticed and were enchanted by the valley climbing up from Pudcombe Cove. They later bought 24 acres and Oswald Milne (assistant to Edward Lutyens) built them a holiday home, Coleton Fishacre, with the Arts and Crafts Movement in mind and an Art Deco interior. We decided to visit the house which is now owned by the National Trust and spent a few hours exploring the house and gardens, and having a light lunch in the café.

Again we resumed our walk and eventually came to rest near Man Sands in a valley between the cliffs. In the night Richard succumbed to the same illness that had struck Celia in Dartmouth. But now we were near Brixham. We called a taxi on our mobile phone but the driver would not come on the farm track, and Richard felt unable to walk to the road. So Celia went to Southdown Farm for help.

The kind farmer's wife arrived at the tent in her Land Rover. With great tenderness and kindness she drove us the few miles to Grenville House, the Outdoor Activity Centre where the Church Lads' and Church Girls' Brigade were going to spend their week's holiday. It was Saturday 21 August and the Brigade arrived that evening. Richard went straight to bed and recovered after two days.

In search of tomatoes

Celia makes a really good pizza on an open cooker when we are camping. Richard fancied a pizza when we were staying in the campervan in Foyers on the south side of Loch Ness in August 1997. Celia didn't have a tin of tomatoes. We climbed up the steep sides of the valley to a little shop 100 metres above the camp-site. No tomatoes.

"Never mind," said Richard, "We'll sail down to Fort Augustus and buy some there."

We had obtained permission to leave our GP14 sailing dinghy, that we had imaginatively called *Boat*, on some land at the loch side. We gathered our gear and launched the dinghy. There was a nice force 3 breeze blowing up the loch which would be against us going, but hopefully would assist us coming back. So we tacked in the sunshine slowly down the loch.

The voyage was about 12 miles each way and took some time. It was becoming late and we knew that our evening meal would be delayed. Slowly we neared the jetty where many pleasure boats were moored. We wondered where we could conveniently stop. The jetty was alongside a fairly narrow river. Suddenly, without warning, the wind changed. It reversed direction and doubled in strength. Loch Ness, being in a deep straight-sided valley has only two directions of wind: up the loch and down the loch.

If you are not used to sailing you may wonder why we didn't continue our journey and buy the tomatoes. The end of the loch had now become a lee shore. The wind was blowing on to it. Lee shores are dangerous. The boat is much more difficult to control and it is hard to escape from the land. Many a sailing boat has been wrecked on a lee shore.

Our plans changed. We gave up thought of buying tomatoes, reefed the mainsail and put up the storm jib to make the sail area smaller, and set off back up the loch. We were at the south west end of a 24 mile long loch. Soon the strong wind was building up waves which in an hour had become quite big. It was a real struggle sailing against wind and waves. Of course we had to tack again when we had expected a gentle but speedy run before the breeze.

The wind became even stronger and our progress up the loch was very slow. We were not in any danger as long as we kept on sailing, but we were becoming tired. And it was becoming darker. It would be really difficult to find our landing place. Most of Loch Ness is bounded by steep sides composed of large and unforgiving rocks. There is hardly anywhere for a small sailing boat to land. It is also very deep so we could not anchor.

Perhaps we should have had beans on toast!

Just then we noticed, in the gloom, a jetty sticking out into the loch. It was a floating pontoon, fixed at the shore end and stopped from moving sideways by ropes on either side at the loch end. We sailed across to it. The notice read PRIVATE – NO LANDING. It was an emergency and we didn't intend to land – just to tie up to it for a few hours. We came close to it and immediately realised that, since it was going up and down violently with the large waves, if we tied the dinghy to it, it would smash the boat.

So we moved Boat along the rope securing the jetty. The rope was slimy and covered in weed but we held on to it. We did not know a knot that would keep us secured safely so we held on to it by hand – and we held it all night! Our arms provided springiness so that the boat was not jarred. The constant motion kept us awake. At one time it began to rain so we covered ourselves with the sail. We played the game thinking of animals beginning with A, B, C etc (Alligator, Badger, Cat) and then vegetables (Artichoke, Beetroot, Cabbage) and so on; and we held on!

Fortunately the summer nights in Scotland are short. It began to get light. At 4 o'clock we decided to sail home. So we hoisted the sails and let go. It was still very windy and great waves were coming down Loch Ness. We saw a fisherman on the shore. A yacht came motoring down the loch. Goodness knows what they thought we were doing! But it was light and by 6.00 am we were back at our landing place – very cold indeed.

We pulled the boat ashore and returned to the campervan. One of its great features was a gas-powered hot air blower which we put on full. We were soon dry; a bit tired, but warm. Whatever we had for breakfast it didn't have any tomatoes in it.

Circumnavigating the Great Lakes

We spent 5 weeks in North America. First we visited Greg and Laurel Diehl in Boston. Greg kindly took us to Plymouth where we visited a reconstruction of the village built by the Pilgrim Fathers when they arrived in America. Actors took the parts of some of the villagers. They spoke to us and we could question them about their lives. We were impressed with their regional English accents and the way they stayed in character. We also were taken to a baseball match and explored old Boston, following a red line painted on the pavement to stop tourists getting lost.

We flew to Detroit and were met by Greg's father, Henry Diehl who, with his wife Jo, were missionaries in Ghana, close to us in Ho. They had been especially kind to us when Duncan had been born. He took us to their home in Defiance, Ohio. They and their neighbours most kindly lent us a car with a folding caravan which they had filled with food. We drove it along the southern shore of Lake Erie to the Niagara Falls. There we camped and were impressed by the grandeur and beauty of the waterfalls.

The following day we drove up to Haliburton in Ontario Canada, where other neighbours from Ghana, Kathy and John Stouffer, lived. They lent us a canoe and took us a few miles north to a regional park and left us for a few days staying in the folding caravan on a pitch by a lake. We enjoyed listening to and watching Great Northern Divers on the lake and the antics of chipmunks round the caravan. While we were canoeing we saw a beaver dam and lodge.

Then we set off north and west past Georgian Bay and the north of Lake Superior; then across the Mississippi River to Iowa and East to Chicago before returning to the Diehl's in Defiance. We drove about 100 miles a day and explored. Everywhere we went we looked at things and talked to people: Native American wall paintings and burial mounds in the shapes of birds and animals; Rivers where logs had been brought down in great piles. Coming back into the USA from Canada we somehow managed to get on the American side of the border before we reached the border control. That caused some confusion for the authorities and us.

In the UK on urban motorways the signs on overhead gantries show which lane one should be in to reach a destination. In the USA they indicate the next exit – so the first exit is on the right, the next exit is to the left of it etc. In Chicago we were driving on a many-lane highway in the right-hand lane when we spotted our destination over the other side. Immediately Richard began winking left. The traffic was moving quite fast but was nose to tail. Slowly he manoeuvred the car and caravan across the busy lanes until we were in the left-hand lane. There was no indication that we were not American so we hoped no-one would shoot us. But then (as we passed an exit on the right) the destination we wanted moved one lane to the right. We immediately realised how the system worked. There was no way for it but to move across the other way to the right until we were where we had started. We indicated right and moved back through the same traffic and got some very funny looks from other drivers (though fortunately no shots!).

Eventually we returned to Henry and Jo Diehl in Defiance. It was a Saturday and they were very keen to hear about all our adventures. That night Jo said to us, "We're going out for breakfast so make sure you're up early." We neither understood nor believed her. Going out for breakfast was outside our experience. So we were asleep when at 7.30 am there was a knocking on our bedroom door and a voice saying, "Aren't you guys coming?" We got up quickly and emerged a bit sleepy and confused.

They took us to a restaurant which we were surprised to find very busy. We were even more surprised to find a dozen of their friends who had come out especially to meet us. The Diehl's explained that these were some of the folk who had lent the caravan and kindly contributed food for it. So we had waffles and coffee and told them where we had been, and thanked them profusely.

We went to church where there were more people to meet. We returned to the Diehl's home to find that there was another dozen for lunch. And these also had contributed and were eager to meet us. In the evening there were twelve more folk to talk to with the same rules. We were exhausted!

After a few good days spent with Jo and Henry the plan was that we should fly to Washington DC and spend some days with their daughter Debbie and her husband Peter in Winchester. Unfortunately the airline was on strike.

The airline paid for a hire car and we drove ourselves right across the Blue Ridge Mountains of Virginia to Winchester. On the way we stayed for two nights with my cousin Clare and her family in the Spring Valley Bruderhof, a Christian Community in Farmington, Pennsylvania.

The community had originally been formed after the 1st World War in Germany as a response to that war. Pacifist Christians from various parts of Europe and especially Germany had joined together. When the Nazi Party rose to power in the 1930s, their large house was commandeered and they fled to Birmingham in England. It was there that Clare's mother Sylvia joined them. When the second world war broke out it was not comfortable for a German community to live in England so passage was arranged for them to Paraguay. There Clare grew up but after 20 years the community decided to move to the USA.

When we visited them they had about 300 members living in families. Single folk were assigned to a family if they did not have one of their own. The community had a primary school in which we spent a morning. There were about 80 children. We told them something of our lives in England and they sang us a song. Older children attended the High School outside the community. When school was over, the youngsters returned to their families who spent time with them without there being any distractions. In the evening the whole community ate together in a huge hall. The food was simple. For example, much of the fruit was slightly damaged. One just cut off the spoilt part and rejoiced in what was good.

One of the community's activities was publishing Christian books. We spent a few hours helping pack the books into boxes. The community was happy to use modern things such as the internet and TV, but none of its members owned their personal things. Everything belonged to the community. Adults of all ages were encouraged to take some part in working if they were able. Even Auntie Sylvia, aged 90, worked a little in the laundry. Clare helped her and looked after her. The community owned a few vehicles which were available for members to drive. They had a lake and we saw families swimming and canoeing happily on it after school. We were very impressed. When the Gulf War was happening and American cruise missiles were exploding in Iraq, the community sent 4 members to live in Baghdad and pray for the situation.

We had last seen Debbie in Ghana when she was a tiny baby. She had changed somewhat! It was really kind of her and her brother Greg and their families to put their parents' friends up and entertain them. There was some discussion as to how we should get to Washington. The parents thought it should be the train as we would have a problem parking but Peter and Debbie said they always went by car. So we drove to the capital.

We put the car in a car park near the Potomac River and walked into the centre of the city. We admired the White House and the Capitol Building. We visited the Aeronautical and Space Museum. In the evening we had dinner in a railway station where there was a great number of different food outlets, and then walked back watching a volleyball game on the way. We arrived back at the car park at 7.00 pm and got into the car which would not start.

We decided to ring the National car rental company from whom we had hired the car so set off in search of a public phone. We walked back into the centre of Washington but couldn't find anything looking like a phone booth. Eventually we came to the United States Treasury building. We thought they must have a phone there and went to speak to the man on the barrier. When he heard our story he immediately called for a cop car. Within two minutes a car hurtled up and two policemen jumped out. They also listened to our story, and then invited us to jump in the back of their car.

We learnt what it was like to be guilty unless proved innocent: the backseat had no comfortable padding; the seat belts had locks which we could not undo; there was no way of opening the car doors from the inside. The policemen were very pleasant and apologised for our treatment. We had told them that the car was parked by the Potomac River and they drove us there. We were surprised that there were some roadworks and very rough ground just before the car park which we hadn't remembered when we put the car there. It was very uncomfortable for us in the back. We drove into the car park. Our hire car was not there.

"Don't worry," said the driver, "there are four more car parks, all the same."

"Don't bother about the next three then," we replied, "it will be in the one at the other end."

But they were very thorough and we drove into each car park in turn, carefully surveying it. In the fifth one there was the car. They had some jump leads and spent half an hour not starting it. After a brief conversation they came to us and said that they were going to take us to the National Airport where there would be an office of the rental company. They would not leave us at the car park because they said it was not a safe place at night. So we drove in the uncomfortable police car over the Potomac River to the National Airport.

The police parked outside the National Car Rental office and sent us inside. We explained the problem and the employee was probably working towards a solution, but he was rather slow. All at once one of the cops stormed in shouting, "these people have come from England to visit our capital city," he thundered, "and you are wrecking their experience. Go and fetch your boss."

We were quite embarrassed. What we had driven in the States so far had been ordinary small family cars. Within a few minutes we had been provided with a huge, top of the range, Buick, which had features we did not know that any car had. Like the other cars it had an automatic gearbox, but Richard had to ask where the gear lever was, (a tiny thing on the steering wheel) and how he switched the lights on (it was automatic). He was impressed (and appalled) by its width. But it had a full tank of gas, free of charge.

The policemen had a brief conversation and asked us to follow them back to the original hire car. By now a tow truck had arrived and the procession of three vehicles began to move. Barriers opened and shut allowing us all to proceed. At last we reached the open road. As the police car swung into the centre of the multi-lane highway on came its blue flashing lights and up went its speed. Cars ahead dived out of the way. Richard held on grimly to the steering wheel of the huge unfamiliar car, and the tow truck battled on behind.

We could not imagine what other motorists thought as the police car sped past them, chased by the big Buick and a tow truck. Sometimes their indicating was very late and gave us little chance to wink, before we turned in front of startled drivers. Eventually the nightmare ended and we arrived back in the car park. We rescued our luggage and placed it in the cavernous boot (*trunk* since we were in the U S A). The tow truck attended to the broken down car and we said fond farewells with grateful thanks to the policemen. They asked for our address in England so they could write to us. (We never heard from them).

As soon as they had left us they returned with the question, "Do you know the way to the road to Winchester?"

We told them we didn't and immediately regretted it. "Follow us!" They said.

So we had a repeat performance only this time without the tow truck. At last they pulled over to the right and we stopped behind them. More farewells.

"Drive to the next junction, turn left, and that's the road to Winchester.

We drove to the next junction where we saw the sign: No left turn! What were we to do? If we didn't turn left we would have another visit from our friendly policemen. If we turned left we might find a different blue flashing light on our tail. We turned left and were on our way to Winchester.

We had told Debbie and Peter that we would be back before it was dark but the sun had set some hours ago. We realised we should have phoned from the rental company office but we hadn't. This was before the days of mobile phones so we needed to find a public phone. But we were on a main road. Then we saw a sign pointing towards Dulles International Airport. The airport was more or less on our way. There must be a phone we could use there!

The reader ought to know (which we didn't) that the Dulles Access Road is a four-lane, 13.65-mile (21.97 km) highway that runs "inside" the Dulles Toll Road along its centre. There are no general-access exits from the west-bound lanes, and no general-access entrances to the east-bound lanes, with the exception of gated slip ramps to and from the toll road that buses and emergency vehicles can use. The Access Road was built as part of the construction of Dulles Airport, and opened with the airport in 1962.

As we speeded up the road we noticed that there didn't seem to be any exits, and that therefore we had no choice but to continue. We arrived at the airport but somehow we must have taken a wrong turn. We could see terminal buildings in the far distance but we couldn't get to them. On and on we drove. Then we saw a taxi and decided to follow it. Perhaps it was going to a terminal building. Eventually we reached a barrier and drove into a car park full of taxis. The attendant on the barrier looked surprised when we passed. We realised that the taxi was being put to bed for the night so we went out of the barrier again, giving a wave to the attendant.

We should have asked the attendant where we could phone – but it was getting really late now and we decided to cut our losses and get to Winchester as soon as possible. We continued driving until we found a sign which said exit. There were several more such signs before we found ourselves on a proper road again. We were surprised that we hadn't been offered any choice of destination – and then the knowledge hit us: we were on the same road back to Washington, and just as we had no exits coming so we had no exits going back!

After a couple of miles we saw a police car parked on the side of the road and we pulled up behind it. The cop was speaking to a driver in a car in front. Five minutes passed and we thought that perhaps there was another officer in the car who we could speak to. Richard got out of the car and took one step towards the police car.

"Get back into your car!" yelled the policeman, and pointed his gun at Richard.

He got back into the car!

After a few minutes he came up to us warily.

"Nobody creeps up on me in the dark", he said. "What do you want?"

We left out most of the story and just explained that we were lost and trying to get to Winchester. His face fell. It must have been obvious that we were British and that may have helped us. He spoke into his radio.

"This is what I want you to do," he said, "Pull off the road and drive across that land. At the other side is a road. Turn right. That is the road to Winchester."

We did as he instructed and arrived at Peter and Debbie's home about 2.00 am. He, a doctor, had phoned every emergency hospital in Washington DC to ask if we had been brought in. Jo and Henry had rung them at 7.00 pm to find out if we had had a good day. They rang again at 9.30 pm. Their daughter told them she would ring when she had any news. They were all remarkably forgiving of us – even quite sympathetic.

Flying

Richard always wanted to fly. His uncle Eric took him up in a Dragon Rapide, a biplane, which cost two and six (12½p) at Ringway Aerodrome (now Manchester International Airport) when he was six.

Commercial aircraft never excited him very much. He does not enjoy the crowded cabin atmosphere of a passenger flight, though we both like looking out of the window: the bright clouds seen from above; occasional glimpses of the ground, sometimes familiar places seen as from Google Earth. There have been special views: the icy mountains of Greenland when we were on our way to the United States; the shining ribbon of the River Niger as we approached Ghana after flying across the Sahara; the Atlas Mountains topped with snow as we travelled down the African coast on our way to the Gambia; the coast of Chile with places we had spent days exploring as we returned from Puerto Montt to Santiago when we visited our son Justin. These are unforgettable memories.

But what inspired Richard was the thought of soaring in the sky alone and free.

His mother suffered various experiments which his teenage years required. Most involved his friend Christopher, who later became his stepbrother. They tried to develop rocket engines. It was fortunate that the garage was made of asbestos as it was the scene of various fires and explosions. His mother's pantry contained a Winchester quart of concentrated nitric acid for some months. It was fortunate that it never got anywhere near the petrol it was intended for.

Probably the earliest flying was Chris and Richard's balloon launching phase. At the time the gas provided through the main was from burning coal to form coke. Unlike natural gas it was lighter than air. Out of a bicycle pump they made a very crude (and dangerously leaky) pump to inflate party balloons with coal gas. They and this apparatus not only managed to survive in the kitchen, but also pumped up about 30 buoyant balloons. Labels were attached and they were sent off into the sky. They were launched from Richard's home in Reigate in Surrey and replies were received from three. One person in Ghent, Belgium, described how he had seen the balloon floating down as he worked in his garden in the morning. He "hoped us to win our competition". Another balloon travelled to Paris while the furthest flew 600 miles (960km) to Rodez in the South of France.

As a teenager Richard made several balsawood model aircraft, both gliders and those propelled by rubber bands. But he had not much flying joy with these. Duncan, our elder son, built a radio controlled model glider when we lived in Guildford. We flew it together on the North Downs and then he sold it to Richard when he went to university. At first Richard found it difficult to see which way it was flying, or tell how far away it was, but eventually he became moderately competent at controlling it and landing it fairly nearby. We flew it on the South Downs near Lancing and at Devil's Dyke, north of Hove. Once he kept it airborne for over an hour; once he followed a group of gulls in a thermal; once we spent several hours looking for it when it landed out of sight.

In his imagination he was flying up in the sky with it.

In May 1995 we stayed in our campervan at Little Hucklow near Tideswell in Derbyshire. Right over our heads sailplanes were being launched from the Derbyshire & Lancashire Gliding Club at Camphill. We booked for a week's instruction and returned to the gliding field the following May.

It was exciting and we became adept at driving the tractors used for towing the gliders from landing site to launch site. But, because the weather was not very good, and the group being taught was quite large, our time in the air was short and at the controls even shorter. We felt that the tuition was poor and there was too little attention to safety. We wrote telling the club our feelings on these matters and were invited to write in greater detail. We made the criticisms as beneficial to the club as possible. As a thank you we were invited for a day's flying with the Chief Instructor.

Apart from these problems we decided that the learning curve for fixed wing flying was too shallow for us. To progress to any expertise we would have had to commit a great deal of time and money to the enterprise.

Then in August 2000 we spent a holiday in Talybont on Usk in South Wales. We saw paragliders flying from the Blorenge near Abergavenny and discovered Paraventure Extreme Sports. On our return we found their website and booked into Club Pilot courses for the following summer.

We spent 4 weeks in the area with the hope of having enough flyable days to complete the course. In the event the whole of Britain was afflicted by foot and mouth disease and the restrictions in place stopped us and others exploring the countryside, and reduced greatly the number of flyable sites.

But on 25 July 2001 we assembled at Abergavenny Railway Station with a few others. We were by far the oldest but the instructors assured us that this was no problem, so long as we could carry the paragliders up the hill.

We drove in convoy to Blaenavon, were taught and practised the parachute landing fall, and then introduced to the paraglider. We learnt the checks that we needed to make at regular intervals, and before every flight. We walked a short distance up the hill and laid the wing out on the ground. There was no wind. We put our helmets on and got into the harnesses. Some people managed the forward launch and a short flight first-time. Celia was airborne after a few tries. Richard spent the rest of the day running down the hill, but never going fast enough to achieve takeoff speed.

Two days later we were back at Blaenavon. This time there was a light wind on to the slope which was helpful because it reduced the speed at which we had to run. We managed four short flights, each time increasing our take-off height. We practiced some S-turns on the way down, which had the unintended effect of shortening the flight and making the following climb not so far.

There was further flying practice on the 31st July and the 7th August, this time at Fochriw, because the wind was in a different direction. We began to learn the reverse launch.

On 17 August 2001 we took our Elementary Pilot theory exam and both got 100%. In spite of the restrictions because of foot and mouth we were making some progress.

During the rest of 2001, and in 2002, we travelled down to South Wales whenever it seemed that the Mondays were going to be flyable. We made our first soaring flights at Treorchy on 4 March 2002, which were very exhilarating. Following that we bought our own gliders and harnesses. There were days when we travelled all the way down to South Wales from the Midlands only to sit about on a hill because the conditions were not right. Sometimes we moved to another hill but the wind was still not right. On 15 April 2002 we travelled to Hay Bluff but found there was not enough wind so everyone else went to the pub while we had lunch in our camper and checked our new gliders. There was a slight breeze in the late afternoon. The other folks returned from the pub and several, including Celia, got into the air but when it was Richard's turn the wind had dropped and he just went down!

On 15 July 2002 we returned to Blaenavon in South Wales and had just one flight after a forward launch. It was a wonderful soaring flight reaching 200 feet above take-off level. We could see the scarp below us and people with their paragliders on top of the hill. Richard landed nearby and walked the glider, still inflated, back to the launch site. Celia reported that she had seen a kestrel hovering beneath her when it was her turn. The dream of soaring in the sky alone and free was beginning to be realised.

Two weeks later we were back in Fochriw. We began to be given tasks which we had to do to complete our Club Pilot award. After taking off with reverse launches Richard had to gain a good height and then collapse part of the wing. The first, called *Big Ears*, involved collapsing the ends of the wings to enable the glider to lose height quickly. The second, an asymmetric tuck, meant he had to collapse the end of just one wing. This is something which can happen when you're not expecting it, if, for example, the air is turbulent. You have to demonstrate that you can handle it if the wing collapses unexpectedly. When you collapse the end of one wing, the glider immediately begins to turn in that direction. If no correction is made the glider can go into a spin. We had to hold the glider in straight flight by braking with the line on the opposite side to the collapse. When the glider was under control we could pull firmly on the other brake to re-inflate the wing, though our gliders were very friendly and tended to re-inflate by themselves.

At this time we were busy with ministry. We had little free time but when the weather was at all flyable on days off we headed to South Wales. We should have done much more ground handling: practising inflating and controlling the glider on the ground. We were a little shy and didn't want to be seen doing this around Bradley. Sometimes on a Monday we did take the paragliders into the country to practise on the ground but we never found a place with a really smooth airflow. Once we took them on to the Long Mynd and found a good open place, but were invited by a warden to go elsewhere where paragliding was allowed. But we were ground-handling and not intending to fly. We twice went to a recreation ground in a Staffordshire village but were stopped by an officer of the parish council who was concerned about insurance. Our membership of the British Hang Gliding and Paragliding Association provides third-party insurance but he didn't seem impressed by that.

We decided to spend a week in the French Alps where, we were told, the weather would be much more settled, and we could give much more time to flying and practising. We were also told that we could finish our Club Pilot qualification. In July 2003 we crossed from Poole to Cherbourg, drove through France, and stayed with John, one of the instructors from Paraventure Extreme Sports with whom we had flown at Fochriw, who was renting a chalet in a valley above Bourg St. Maurice.

This is a winter sports area though now it was of course summer. We could not believe how steep the snowless ski run was from which we were to take off. Richard was scared, though later he saw that place as quite benign when we used what John called "committed take-offs". At one of these he said to Richard, "Make sure your glider is properly inflated before you launch. You are going off a 1000 ft. cliff and if it is not properly inflated you will not survive."

We were not doing daredevil tricks. John was a qualified BHPA instructor who reminded us of the seriousness of what we were doing and enabled us to do it safely.

On our first day of flying Richard pulled up over his head the glider, which had been laid out behind him, and ran down the steep slope between the woods of fir trees on either side. After a few steps he fell over and had to carry the glider back up the hill. He eventually launched more or less successfully at the third attempt.

"I was in the air and settling into the comfort of the harness. I applied a little right brake to avoid Café Felix at the bottom of the slope, and moved to the right, over the trees. Soon I was about 200 ft. over the rooftops of the small village of Vallandry.

Then I found myself high over the trees on the sides of the Isère Valley. There was no breeze and no lift so I began a long and pleasant glide down to the landing field that we had been shown the day before. I was still fairly high when I reached it so I followed other gliders along the right-hand side, turned at the other end, and made quite a nice landing in the middle of the field." Celia did similarly.

John collected us and within an hour we were taking off again from the same ski run. This time the launch was something of a slalom as Richard kept over-correcting but he got airborne on the first attempt. Again he moved over Vallandry but this time his vario began beeping with increasing pitch indicating that he was rising. After two seconds he turned and continued circulating to try to stay in the rising air. This was the first time that he had done 360 degree turns. His vario indicated that he had risen 957 ft.

Celia coming in to land at Bourg St Maurice

This was all a new experience for us and we found it very exciting. We were each sitting high in the sky in a harness which was like a comfortable armchair with nothing around us and the ground a very long way beneath. There were other gliders in the air too so we had to make sure we obeyed the rules of the air to keep out of their way. After a little searching, Richard saw Celia a little lower down and nearer the landing field. He set off for the landing field at Bourg St. Maurice and arrived quite high up. He did a 360 degree turn in order to lose height. John had warned us that there would be a breeze along the valley and it was important we look at the wind sock and land into the wind. So Richard again flew to the other end and turned towards the field. He was still too high and so did an S-turn to lose height and then landed near the middle of the field.

This was a period in which Europe was experiencing a heatwave. Hundreds of elderly people in France died from the high temperatures. We spent most afternoons practising ground handling and found it exhausting.

On the first of August we travelled towards Bourg St Maurice and up to Le Fort de La Platte which has an altitude of 1960 metres. Richard launched at the first attempt. He found launching much easier after he discovered that you don't have to run until the canopy is inflated. Soon after take-off he found his camera, which had been in his pocket, unattached on his lap! The obvious rule is that everything has to be tied on! He was very fortunate that the camera hadn't fallen to the ground. He took the photo on the next page and then tied the camera on!

There was some valley breeze against him so he made slow progress towards the landing field. John had stayed at the landing field as he wanted to see us do asymmetric tucks and big ears. When we did these in South Wales we were only 200 ft. above the instructor. We had to hold the position for about four seconds. He indicated with his arm when he was satisfied. Here in France we were very much higher so we could not see John. We communicated by radio. Richard did right hand and left hand 50% asymmetric tucks. In other words he collapsed half the wing and flew for a few seconds on the remaining half. It was much more tippy than the 30% one he did in Wales, and more difficult to maintain course. Then he collapsed both ends of the wing and held the resulting *Big Ears* for several seconds to lose height. After two 360s and an S-turn he landed facing away from Bourg.

The best time for flying in the Alps is usually in the evening. Cool air begins to flow down the mountainsides and is warmed by the hot valley floor. The air in the valley then becomes very

173

buoyant and is excellent for paragliding. The problem is that the valley breeze can be quite strong at first and landing difficult. We went to the ski run where we had first launched. John asked us if we could stay up for at least an hour, to give time for the valley breeze to die down a bit. We said we would do our best. As Richard flew over Vallandry he was a little concerned because he seemed to be losing height but as he moved out over the main valley his vario became excited and he gained height. He moved out over a rocky spur towards Landry and did 360s in a powerful thermal.

John had shown us a field in the valley above the chalet where we could land. After Richard had gained quite a lot of height he wondered if he could get back to this field. When he decided that he was high enough and began to move up the valley Richard found himself losing height rather quickly and so returned to the main valley to gain more height. He had been flying for almost an hour and a half and the air seemed much less buoyant so he headed for the landing field near Bourg St Maurice.

After doing a 360 to lose height Richard decided to fly at the left-hand side of the landing field over the River Isère. He could see people doing white water rafting beneath him. The air became very bumpy on this side probably because the valley breeze was passing over a spur. He decided to move to the other side of the landing field. It was bumpy there too but it became smoother as he lost height. Half way down the field he turned to the centre, did an S turn and landed nicely.

Richard walked over to try to find Celia. He found John being spoken to by a Frenchman who told him that she didn't have proper control of the glider and shouldn't be flying. Richard found her sitting in the adjacent field quite upset. On take-off, just as the canopy was overhead and she had begun running, her right wrist was snapped back and she was jerked to the right. She probably should have aborted the take-off but managed to gain control and fly out over Vallandry. She realised that her wrist was hurting badly but John had told us to stay up for at least an hour because of the valley wind. She soared for a while but couldn't bear the pain involved in controlling the wing and so headed for the landing field. It was difficult for her to control the glider but she eventually landed in the field next to the landing field. We had been told we could use it in an emergency.

As she was sitting recovering from the ordeal the Frenchman came up to her and began grumbling at her. He could have asked her what the problem was and been helpful. His only thought was to complain. She had actually broken her wrist and was not able to fly after that while we were in France. Richard wanted to stop flying but Celia was insistent that he carry on, which he did on condition that John arrange for her to be taken tandem flying if she wished. Jules Brown, an expert cross-country pilot, took her up several times.

Two days later Richard had a Frenchman shouting at him. He was flying in the evening and enjoying the very buoyant air. There were many gliders in the air so he kept a good lookout. He had been flying for about half an hour when he found a nice thermal south of Vallandry. He was circling and hoping to gain enough height to fly back to the chalet when he saw another paraglider heading straight for him. Richard continued to circle and was well above the Frenchman when he reached where Richard had been. He obviously thought Richard should have left the thermal and passed on his left, which would have been correct if Richard had not been rising and therefore not in his way.

"He joined the thermal below me shouting at me at the top of his voice."

After a while the Frenchman went away.

Richard didn't gain enough height to fly back to the chalet and so eventually flew to the landing field, did big ears, 360s and S-turns in order to lose height. Normally on landing one pulls on both brakes firmly to stall the glider. This is called flaring. On this occasion Richard was still upset by the Frenchman shouting at him and he flared as he went past the windsock even though he was still several metres off the ground. Fortunately the wing was kind and put him down gently. Richard walked over to John and found the Frenchman complaining to him. He was glad to be able to tell John his side of the story.

A few days later we went in a gondola from Arc 1800 to the Aiguille Grive. This is 2372 m high. We had to walk up the final 100 metres to the summit, a little short of air. A young student Alex had joined us for the week and Jules was with us too. What John described as a committed take-off was required because there was only a short run before a steep cliff. Alex took off first and found lift quickly. Then Richard took off but found no lift at all. Disappointed, he descended all the way down to the Nancroix landing field above the chalet. John came to meet him as he walked on the road down to the chalet.

That evening there was a huge electric storm which caused a landslide up the valley from the chalet. The stream became a heaving mass of mud and rocks. We don't think any property was damaged or anyone was injured, but the road was blocked and impassable.

The following day we repeated the adventure. This time Richard found the final 100 metre climb very tiring. Again Jules and Alex were there. They took off but didn't immediately find lift. When it was his turn Richard found it was bumpy over the ridge but didn't seem able to turn it into lift. He continued further out, beginning to sink and thinking it would be a repeat of the previous day. But he entered a thermal and after a few seconds began to circle. He tried to discover the fastest lift and did many 360s ascending to 8960 feet. Alex and Jules came under him in this thermal. Then Richard came out of the thermal and could not find it again. He moved towards Vallandry and gained some more height in another thermal. He probably should have returned towards the Aiguille Grive but was thinking of crossing the valley which had been suggested if we had enough height. With quite a lot of height he moved over the valley but found bad sink. He searched for lift lower down but didn't find any and intended to land at the upper Nancroix field. Richard could see that it was covered in mud and stones from the previous night's landslide so he decided to land by the small windsock outside the chalet. John was thrilled with Richard's flight, and he was quite pleased himself!

We had several more flights in France. One was more exciting than intended when Richard tried an experiment and went into a spin. The trees below were spinning round and coming towards him quickly. Fortunately he had been very high having taken off above Arc 2000. He used one brake to stop the rotation and both brakes gently to stop the wing stalling. The glider was again friendly and he landed safely at the main landing field. Alex who had taken off before him asked how he had got down so quickly!

Back in England we travelled down to Abergavenny one Monday and successfully completed our Club Pilot exam.

When we moved to Scotland we spent 3 weeks on the Isle of Arran with a small instructor called Zabdi Keen. We were not able to do very much because wewere very rusty and either the wind was too strong for flying or too weak for practising reverse launching. Near our home in Largs is Kaim Hill. Once Richard flew from top to bottom, back to the vehicle. We shall have to see what flying is in store for us in the future. Perhaps it is time to retire? We are very glad and feel so fortunate to have been able to soar in the sky alone and free.

A small TV company were making a film about the Gower Peninsula in South Wales. They wanted to include people who came from other parts of the United Kingdom to explore and enjoy what it offered. They approached Paraventure and were referred to us. They were intrigued by a paragliding vicar.

They spent a Sunday with us in Bradley filming the worship and then coming with Richard on a visit to a couple being prepared for the baptism of their baby. Later we met the TV crew at Rossili Downs in the hope of them being able to film us flying.

Sadly the conditions were too strong and gusty for us though some more experienced people were flying and the lady working the camera was taken up on a tandem paraglider to film from the air. Richard told them that paragliding was like that. Sometimes the best decision you made was not to fly. It is better being on the ground wishing you were in the air than in the air wishing you were on the ground. He also drew their attention to Isaiah 40:28-31

Do you not know? Have you not heard?
The LORD is the everlasting God,
the Creator of the ends of the earth.
He will not grow tired or weary,
and his understanding no-one can fathom.

He gives strength to the weary
and increases the power of the weak.
Even youths grow tired and weary,
and young men stumble and fall;
but those who hope in the LORD
will renew their strength.
They will soar on wings like eagles;
they will run and not grow weary,
they will walk and not be faint.

The programme was shown on HTV (Welsh ITV) and we thought nobody who knew us would see it. We were wrong. Several relatives of our church members lived in Wales and some Bradley folk were on holiday in Wales. We received a few excited reports.

Delving in the past

We have always enjoyed watching the Channel 4 programme *Time Team*. Each episode features an archaeological dig of just 3 days. Some of the sites are well-known for their archaeology, others are just places where there is a feature such as a pile of stones or crop marks. Sometimes a member of the public invites the team into their garden or locality to help solve something which puzzles them.

We have watched so many episodes that we feel we know the individual members of the team. We were very interested then when they shared the idea of the Big Dig. Members of the public were invited to register, do research, and then dig a test pit just one metre square, as a proper piece of archaeology. We invited three other members of St Martin's Church, Bradley to join us on Saturday 26 June 2004 for our own Big Dig. The report of the dig which appeared on the Channel 4 Big Dig website follows:-

The "archaeologists" in discussion

179

INTRODUCTION

Grid reference: SO955955 Excavation by Celia and Richard Walker, Pauline and Terry Calloway and Rosemary Preston. The pit is in the garden of a Victorian Vicarage that was demolished in 1964. Bradley is recorded in the Domesday Book, and there are records of a medieval manor house in the parish. In the 1760s John Wilkinson bought the manor and built the first foundry in the Black Country. His third foundry was only 100 metres from the vicarage. The area was one of intense mining and metal-working until the 1980s. People living in Bradley today are very interested in the recent past. We are hoping to find artefacts which show something of life in Bradley before this. We chose to dig the pit outside the former vicarage, hoping to find some less disturbed ground.

THE LANDSCAPE

Our test pit was excavated in the Bradley Vicarage garden in the heart of the West Midlands conurbation. The site is at about 500 feet near the top of a small hill which gives views over the industrial and post industrial landscape of the Black Country Boroughs and as far as Birmingham 12 miles away.

PRE-EXCAVATION RESEARCH

We looked at a *History of Bilston* [7] by G T Lawley, and *John Wilkinson* [8] by Ron Davies; also Ordnance Survey maps from 1901 and 1938, and earlier 18th and 19th century sketch maps. From these we located the old vicarage roughly and then found marks on the dry ground which located it exactly. From the books we learned that John Wilkinson had built his 3rd foundry about 100 metres South of our site. He bought the manor in 1766 and built a house which we think was probably about 400 metres South west. He also established a pottery 100 metres north-east. The early sketch maps show nothing on the site of our test pit. A vicarage was built close by in 1866 when St Martin's Church was opened a few metres to the West.

Celia recording a context

THE EXCAVATION

The excavation was hand dug with trowels. There were no finds visible on the turf surface or immediately underneath it. Almost immediately under that was a complicated feature of wood, paper and metal finds, with evidence of some burning. Some of this remained to be excavated when the base of context 1 was reached. Other finds at this level included several pieces of clinker, tile, plaster or mortar and pottery.

CONTEXT 2 The wood and metal finds were lifted. Small tree roots were cut off. Other finds were similar to context 1.

CONTEXT 3 There was evidence of brick dust, brick pieces and a piece of drainage pipe was found.

CONTEXT 4 Blue clay (natural?) and brick dust. Bedded into this was a broken drainage pipe or sewer. We thought that below this was the natural soil.

FINDS

BONES - 2 small pieces

POTTERY - 43 fragments - most appeared to be 19th or 20th century of different colours and designs. Two from context 2 were identified by Jane Stewart (JS), on a visit to Birmingham Museum, as Midlands Whiteware 18th or 19th century. One piece from context 4 was described (JS) as possibly the oldest piece we had found. It had a pinky-red fabric containing white granular pieces. One side was dark brown and the other like the fabric but smoother. We intend to take the pottery to the museum in Stoke-on-Trent. Pieces of clay pipe from contexts 2 and 3.

TILE - Various pieces - some modern glazed and some quarry tile. One beautiful tile glazed all over in a rich brown with green and yellow patches. 90mm square, 30mm deep was identified as medieval, possibly 14th or 15th century (JS). The design was in the same yellow colour: a circle enclosing a compass type pattern with 8 "petals" and 8 triangles in the spaces between.

The Medieval tile

182

We have seen similar tiles in Birmingham Museum but neither there, nor in books, with the same design.

GLASS - Ten fragments of glass with various colours and ages. The largest was thick and heavy, dark greeny-brown - possibly the base of a chemist's jar (JS).

METAL - 21 finds: all but two were rusted. 4 appeared to be window fittings, one the wheel of a pipe valve, a hook and length of wire. There were 5 or 6 possible nails. Also a battery contact and modern can ring pull. These last were from contexts 3 and 2 and illustrated that the ground had been disturbed probably by the digging of the sewer/drain. The burnt paper and wood in context 1 may have been from the demolition of the vicarage. In context 3 we found a worked flint, 20mm by 7mm, pointed at one end and flat at the other. It is curved along its length.

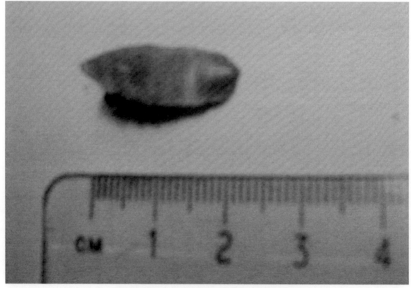

The Mesolithic worked flint

JS thought it was Mesolithic. Pieces of mortar and slag/clinker were found in contexts 2 to 4.

CONCLUSION

The presence of the sewage or drain pipe on the natural layer indicates that the site had been disturbed. Presumably the depth of finds gave no clues as to the time they had been deposited. We were not surprised to find Victorian things such as pottery and clay pipes but we were surprised to find the medieval tile and the Mesolithic worked flint.

It seems to us that there are two options about these very old things:

1. There has been occupation in prehistoric times and medieval times (perhaps even a medieval hall), or

2. A collector (possibly a former vicar) obtained these old things from elsewhere and they became lost here subsequently.

We hope to have time in the future to dig a second pit nearby to see if there are more very old finds. We also intend to show all our finds to JS and take the pottery to Stoke-on-Trent Museum for them to see.

In fact, we retired and left the vicarage, and so we did no further investigation. All the finds were left in the vicarage in the care of our successor.

Walkers on More Water

In the wake of the Vikings

In 1263, the year of the final battle, in Largs, involving the Vikings on mainland Britain, 60 Viking boats sailed to Arrochar up the Firth of Clyde and Loch Long. The ships were hauled overland to Tarbet and relaunched in Loch Lomond and created havoc along its shores.

On Monday 4 June 2007 we noticed a forecast of benign weather for the next 5 days, so we got up early the following morning, trundled our open canoe along the promenade and launched her from a slipway at 7.00 am.

As we left we heard a great splash behind us as a seal slapped the water to see us off. There was slightly more wind against us than we had expected and we made slow progress along the Largs seafront. The ferries to Cumbrae were working but were no problem to us as we crossed their path. We stayed fairly close to the shore to get some shelter from the breeze, and so were able to hear as well as see the vehicles of those on their way to work.

We saw the posts, one near the shore and the other behind it, which mark each end of the Skelmorlie Measured Mile. Many of the great and lesser ships built on the Clyde had their sea trials in the Firth and were brought up to full speed past this nautical mile - first in one direction and then the opposite way to take account of tides.

As we passed over the clear water Celia pointed out a star fish on the rocks below.

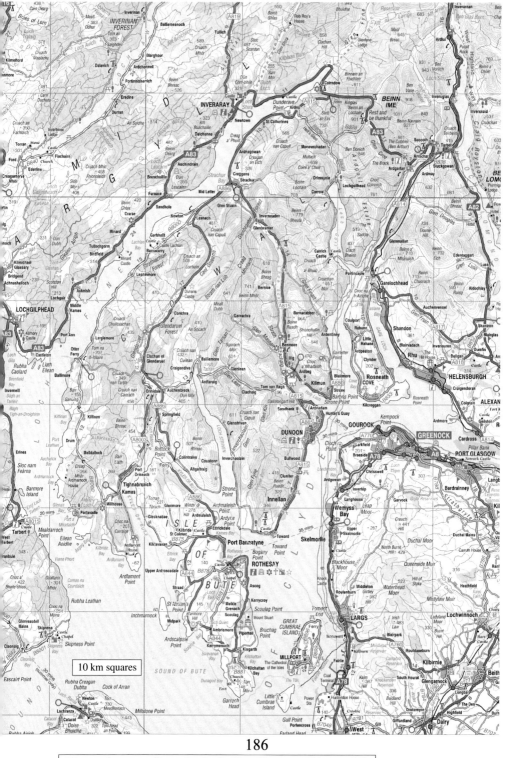

10 km squares

186

Use a magnifying glass to examine these maps. Red tracks - canoe.
Green tracks - sailing dinghy. Black and green – sailing dinghy and lifeboat

We landed at Wemyss Bay near the Rothesay Ferry Terminal and boiled a kettle for a cup of coffee. Then we slipped round the quay ahead of an incoming ferry and resumed our journey. We came to Inverkip Power Station which was Scotland's first oil-fired power station, with construction beginning in 1970. The station is a noted landmark, with its 213m (700-foot) chimney. The plant was designed to produce 1900 mega-watts of electricity but, due to the cost of oil, it has not worked at full capacity, except during the 1984 miner's strike. It stopped generating electricity in the late 1980s and today is maintained only as a strategic reserve, with an uncertain future.

We paddled under the jetty intended for unloading the oil and headed across the Clyde directly towards Dunoon, four and a half miles away. The water was fairly smooth. There was no serious shipping about – only a pair of motor cruisers which turned away when they spotted us and a fishing boat on the north side. A Calmac ferry apparently on its way to Dunoon turned and headed back to Gourock. (Surely not because of us!) Slowly Dunoon came nearer.

We passed the Cowal red and white striped pillar buoy which shows the ships they can pass either side. It is effectively the junction of the Skelmorlie Channel and the Firth of Clyde Channel. We arrived at the Gantocks, rocks exposed at low water, on which the famous paddle steamer *Waverley* went aground on 15 July 1977. We left them and their small lighthouse, to starboard, and passed close to Dunoon Pier. Landing on the beach beyond we pulled the canoe up away from the water.

It had become a grey and fairly cool day with little breeze. We sat on a rock and had lunch. Then we returned to the canoe and paddled north. We were soon at Hunter's Quay where we negotiated the track of the four little red Western Ferries from McInroy's Point to the East. While passing Holy Loch, we checked that we had chosen the correct entrance to Loch Long with two fishermen collecting lobster pots.

As we entered Loch Long several porpoises, possibly more than twenty, entertained us with their arcing movements. We eventually camped in a kind farmer's field at Stronchullin Farm overlooking the loch with a lot of sheep and many more midges.

Camping at Stronchullin Farm

Wednesday turned out to be a sunny day with a light breeze. Midges love these conditions. As they clustered round the tent, and around us as we emerged, we decided to have breakfast on the beach, hoping the midges would not be so numerous there. We used the canoe and its wheels to take everything down to the shore on the farm track. We were careful crossing the road though there was not much traffic about at seven o'clock in the morning. Unfortunately the midges thought it was breakfast time for them as well, and so we were quickly back on the loch. Midges don't seem to like deeper water.

Although it is so beautiful, Loch Long is actually a naval dockyard. A navy ship passed us heading north. There was much hammering and banging coming from an auxiliary navy ship on the east shore. Among the trees behind it there were various interesting buildings surrounded by what looked like a very strong and determined fence. Small patrol boats policed the waters. They were clearly aware of us but, since we kept to the western side, did not come close.

We passed the village of Ardentinny on our left with views of the lovely Glen Finart behind. Mist and sunshine, mountains and solitude. A seal popped up to watch and accompany us for a few hundred yards. Other seals were basking on the shore. The scale of the mountains and the loch was so vast it made our progress seem very slow. Eventually we reached the mouth of Loch Goil and paddled in. With its backdrop of mountains it was utterly beautiful. We stopped at a pebbly beach and had some lunch. Afterwards we walked along the shore about half a mile towards Carrick Castle. We hoped that one day we would be able to return to make a proper exploration of Loch Goil.

Carrick Castle and Loch Goil

There was a fresh breeze blowing up Loch Long which produced some rolling waves. These made our exit from Loch Goil slightly awkward while we were sideways on to them, but we eventually rounded the small lighthouse and continued the passage north. On the east side we slowly passed a huge oil storage depot. There were little families of Mergansers and one of Shelduck. We were surprised to see a passenger train high up on the hillside on its journey from Glasgow to the north-west of Scotland.

Loch Long is appropriately named and we were beginning to look for signs of the Caravan and Camping Club site at Ardgartan. We phoned the wardens but, though we told them clearly, they didn't seem to understand that we were coming by canoe on the loch. So they didn't tell us that the campsite had good access on the north side, the further side from us. We paddled round the site but not far enough to see the egress from

191

the loch. We took the canoe across a rocky shore, unloaded the cargo and carried it up the steep bank and over the fence, and then pulled the canoe up as well. It was only when we were shown our pitch that we realised there was a northern entrance from the loch!

Our pitch by the entrance to Loch Long

Although the wardens assured us the site was half empty it seemed quite full to us, mainly with caravans and large tents. A few months earlier, after our voyage from Bradley to Guildford, described in our other book, *Walkers on Water* (see page 232) Richard had written an article for the Caravan and Camping Club in which he had said how much he enjoyed small-tent camping and felt intimidated by the large outfits, with microwave cookers and TVs, which people used nowadays. It had been published this very month in the club magazine, with a cartoon of us paddling the canoe. It was a little unsettling to be recognised by other campers on the site!

The following day we spent on land. Before we were up we saw a fine fox pass a few yards in front of the tent. We walked round the north end of the sea loch to Arrochar. When we were following a pleasant footpath from the campsite through woodland Celia spotted a red squirrel. Eventually we were forced to use the main road which had come from the pass called "Rest and be Thankful".

In Arrochar we enjoyed the views of the surrounding mountains and surveyed the route we would be taking the canoe the following morning. Then we caught a bus back to the campsite using our wonderful free bus passes. In the evening we watched some folk fishing from the shore. We were rewarded with a gift of mackerel, cooked in a little smoker just like the one we use at home.

Friday morning was warm and sunny with a light breeze. We got up early and were welcomed as usual by midges. We packed up the tent without breakfast and by 5.30 am we were paddling across the loch to Arrochar The tide was quite high so we were able to get the canoe easily to the ramp we had spotted the day before. We carried the cargo and then the canoe up the ramp and had a cup of tea. Then we portaged the canoe (on its wheels) to Tarbet. As in the Isle of Harris (see page 86), the name Tarbet (or Tarbert) indicates that it was a narrow strip of land which the Vikings dragged their boats across, between two stretches of water.

The main road was narrow and surprisingly busy so early in the morning, but the good path saved the day and we were soon at Tarbet. Before we launched on Loch Lomond we had breakfast on a seat by the loch side, talking to a lady resident about our expedition. Then we paddled down the Loch. It was calm and still with no-one about except those preparing the cruisers for trips on the loch for coach parties. We stopped at Rowardennan Hotel for soup and salmon rolls. We spotted a seaplane on the loch and watched it take-off. Soon we reached Milarrochy

Caravan and Camping Club site where we were welcomed and given a pitch close to the slipway.

On the Saturday we were waved off by a dad and his two children with whom we had made friends. It was thick mist. So we kept to the edge of the loch and called into Balmaha where we failed to buy some bits for lunch. The sun came out as we canoed down the loch and found the entrance to the Endrick Water. The water was very shallow in that part of the loch but we found a way deep enough to paddle into the river. We have a cousin (first cousin once removed actually), Alison Williams, and her family who live at Croftamie, about 9 miles up the river. Canoeing up the river was quite hard work as the water level was low and it was often flowing fast, especially just before Drymen Bridge. There were hundreds of sand martins nesting in the banks. Many holes had a bunch of little beaks enthusiastically receiving insects from their parents. We phoned Alison who came to Drymen Showground and took our luggage to her home so the canoe was lighter. We continued paddling and walking up the river.

Celia performing tug duty

We accompanied the family to church the next day and set off again after lunch down the river (an easier direction!) back to Loch Lomond. Alison carried the luggage to Drymen Showground where we met her and reloaded the canoe. We camped wild by Loch Lomond in a country park near the south end. Miraculously there seemed to be no midges.

On the Monday morning we set off early (after 5.00 am breakfast) and paddled down to Balloch barrage. A family of mallards on the slipway stayed asleep and undisturbed as we pulled the canoe past them. We portaged the canoe round the weir and then set off down the River Leven.

The frequent rapids made that 7 miles quite exciting. We were pleased to see a dipper fishing in the fast flowing water. We rejoined the Clyde in the sunshine by Dumbarton Rock. It was almost high water on another calm day so we paddled across and along the river to Greenock where we climbed a vertical ladder on to the Waterfront, leaving the loaded canoe moored at the base. As we were eating some fish and chips for lunch, two things happened almost together: Two waterways policemen arrived in their boat. They had noticed us canoeing in the navigation channel and wanted to make sure we were aware of the rules. They were satisfied with our assurance that we were well-qualified and understood the shipping regulations.

Just before we noticed the policemen arriving, a young man walking on the quayside decided to strip off and leap the 20 feet down to the water. As he surfaced he shouted out to his mates, "I've found a canoe – I'm going for a paddle." When we looked over the railings he was sitting astride the canoe and untying it. The police were wonderfully on hand to dissuade him from taking it.

We continued round the coast and got back home to Largs as the sun was setting. Tired! We had covered 33 miles that day and 107 miles in all.

Rescue

We intended to set off in our Wayfarer sailing dinghy on Friday 9 May but delayed because of the blustery wind. The general weather forecast was for light easterly winds for the next few days. We had been making piles of equipment, clothes and food, according to our prepared lists. These were loaded into dry bags so that we could put our hands on anything quickly.

On the Sunday the inshore shipping forecast was for variable force three winds. So we took Squacco to Largs Marina and paid eight pounds for use of the slipway. Having loaded the boat and put it into the water, we rowed it to a pontoon. Richard took the vehicle and trailer back to the house while Celia sorted out the boat.

Eventually we set off at about 11 am. The wind was a light easterly which gave us a choice of direction. We rowed out of the marina, hoisted the sails, and set off towards Arran. After a short distance we noticed that the yachts ahead of us were tacking meaning that the wind would be against us. So we turned round and headed north. The wind was so light and fluky that we thought of mooring at the Sailing Institute. We continued very slowly past Great Cumbrae. The ferry kindly diverted behind us. As we left the island behind, the wind increased a little but it was still very slight.

We met the Largs inshore lifeboat, training. The helmsman said, "It's a lovely day for a sail - pity there is no wind." We have noticed that Scots often say, "See you later!" when they mean, "goodbye", or as the Americans say, "have a nice day." Richard said to the lifeboat men, "See you later!" – But he didn't mean it how it happened!

We continued slowly towards Rothesay. When we were about halfway across, a fresh breeze blew up from the north-east. Celia put up the sprayhood that we had made. We passed a few yachts heading southeast and saw several porpoises arcing in the waves.

The wind dropped as we sailed across Rothesay Sound. We did think about stopping overnight at Rothesay but the wind was just enough to keep us heading gently northwest. Seals popping up to have a look at us, and gannets diving from a height, entertained us. As we passed Ardyne Point the wind got up again. The Pilot had warned us to expect squalls, from Loch Striven, which had been known to overwhelm yachts. As a precaution we put a double reef in the mainsail, but we saw no sign of a squall.

As soon as we entered the East Kyle the easterly returned, force 4 or 5. We were glad of the reduced sail, and enjoyed a splendid open reach meeting several yachts close-hauled.

We passed the Colintraive to Rhubodach ferry (we call it the rubber duck!) and soon came to the Burnt Islands. We elected to go through the more northerly buoyed passage, and then continued more or less straight on behind Eilean Dubh where an anchorage was indicated on the chart.

Approaching the Burnt Islands

We found ourselves in a beautiful spot, surrounded by mountains, rocks and trees, with a few moored small boats, and were joined for the night by a yacht. We put up our boat tent and, after a meal, went to bed.

We woke at 4.30 but didn't get up till seven o'clock. The inshore forecast for the Clyde spoke of light easterly winds – but we knew that the weather here doesn't take any notice of forecasts!

A swan tried, unsuccessfully, to persuade us to share breakfast with him. We don't think it is a good idea to make wild-life associate boats with food. Then we packed up the tent, stowed everything, and set off slowly in the light breeze. We said, "Good Morning" to the four youngsters having breakfast in the cockpit of the yacht and entered the West Kyle.

The wind was from the East, about force 2, so Squacco gentled her way south-west. We passed a fish farm and a man examining lobster pots. Many yachts were anchored off Tighnabruaich. A large police boat was heading north-east.

Passing Tighnabruaich

As we passed Rubha Dubh, turning southeast, and hardening up the sails, the wind increased so much that we decided to double reef again. We were able to do this while being hoved to (stationary with our sails and rudder set in a particular way) for a few minutes.

Our original intention had been to turn west as we left the Kyles of Bute and sail to Portavadie in Loch Fyne. But it was now so windy that we doubted whether we would be able to get back again soon. We continued down the west coast of Bute with the intention of going back to Largs.

As we entered Inchmarnock Sound we decided to seek some shelter from the strong wind, for lunch, in St Ninian's Bay. We tacked up to the north-east corner and laid the anchor. It was very windy and not at all sheltered.

Within a few minutes we found ourselves sailing again. We have a good Fortress anchor and so were surprised it was not holding in the sand. We tacked in again and anchored once more. This time we had about half-an-hour, a cup of tea, a piece of bread and a sardine, before the wind drove the anchor free.

We hoisted the mainsail with its two reefs and set off again. It was very windy – possibly force 5. As we sailed south-west the wind gradually reduced and we enjoyed lovely views of Garroch Head.

Garroch Head

Indeed, at the south end it was quite placid. We sailed across to the western elbow of Little Cumbrae, passing between two big ships coming down the Firth of Clyde Channel.

We headed north up the Firth of Clyde Channel and turned into the Tan passing Millport. At this point we should have made a different decision. We think we should have continued all the way along the western side of Great Cumbrae, and then sailed south-east to Largs Marina. It might have been quite rough off the north side of Cumbrae but nothing like what we met north-east of Little Cumbrae.

It took us a while to tack through the Tan, between the Cumbraes. Then we met a very fierce wind, probably channelled down the Kelburn Valley. Between Great Cumbrae, Wee Cumbrae and Hunterston there was a maelstrom with steep, chaotic waves and winds blustering probably to force 7. Spray was lifting off the white-topped waves. We tried tacking through it, but made no headway. We thought of going south to Ardrossan but knew the entrance had many rocks on its north side. We could not merely run to sea because the Isle of Little Cumbrae was behind us and we were being blown towards it.

At this moment the round turn and two half hitches, which we had mistakenly used to tie the mainsheet to the boom instead of a bowline, came undone, and we were unable to control Squacco.

Richard took the hand-held VHF radio from our grab bag and spoke into it: *Mayday, Mayday, Mayday, this is sailing dinghy Squacco, Mayday.* Immediately the coastguard at Greenock responded. Squacco is registered with the coastguard so as soon as you tell them the name (or in our case spell it out: Sierra, Quebec, Uniform, Alpha, Charlie, Charlie, Oscar) they know what kind of boat you are and what safety gear you carry. They need to know the boat's position, the nature of the distress, the number of people on board.

You say, "I require immediate assistance." (And then you try not to forget to say OVER)

A yacht from Millport came out and threw us a line to hold us off the island. The Largs Inshore Lifeboat arrived soon after. We were pleased to see them!

They asked us to get into the lifeboat, put one of their own men in Squacco and began to tow the dinghy back to Largs. They were concerned that we were cold, and dressed us in jolly yellow plastic bags.

Perhaps they were towing the dinghy too fast in the very buffeting waves. The mast began to swing wildly back and forth and then came down on the lifeboat man. Neither the mast, the boat nor the lifeboat man were seriously damaged, but the mast pivot pin was bent, the genoa furling tube was broken in half, puncturing the genoa, and the burgee was wrecked. We carry a Secumar anti-inversion cushion at the top of the mast. When the mast came down it was an unscheduled test of this air-bag inflation. It was good to see it passed the test with flying colours.

When we arrived in Largs Marina we were met by two coastguards who took us to our home because they were concerned that we were cold. We appreciated their care.

The following morning we returned to the marina to recover the boat and begin putting in operation the repairs and replacements that were necessary. In the afternoon we walked down to the Largs Inshore lifeboat station and thanked the men for their help.

Scotland Coast to Coast – a scenic way

One of the delights of being retired and living on the coast is that you can choose your time to suit the weather. We noticed a fat high pressure system building and decided that 30 May was the day to go. We were up at 4.00am and ready to leave by 5. But it was too windy for our open canoe on the sea. So we waited till the breeze had dropped a little and, after an early lunch, trundled the canoe along the promenade and launched it at a slipway known locally as Cairnie's Quay.

Cairnie's Quay

We had soon left Largs behind and were pleased to meet two boats being rowed from Greenock back home to Millport on the Isle of Cumbrae. It is always good to meet fellow voyagers in small boats.

Having passed across the track of a CalMac Ferry approaching Wemyss Bay from Rothesay we landed on a sandy beach and enjoyed a cup of tea, disappointing a small boy who wanted us to let him paddle the canoe.

Last time we paddled this way we called in at Dunoon but now we headed straight up Loch Long. Some of the time we were 2km from the shores so we kept a good eye out for shipping and for the wind. We wear buoyancy aids and carry two large fenders for buoyancy in the ends of the canoe. All our kit is in dry bags which are well secured and we carry mini-flares, orange smokes, and a VHF radio in a waterproof cask. We are also aware of the direction of the tide so that, in the event of a capsize that we were not able to right, we would be able to swim the boat ashore.

We greeted a fishing boat collecting lobster pots in the entrance to Loch Long and enjoyed the sight of dozens of porpoises, their backs glistening as they arced in the sunlight.

About 5km up Loch Long we stopped on the west shore, pitched our little tent on the beach, and made our evening meal on our Trangia gas stove. One of the joys of exploring is the people we meet and chat to. Here a young woman arrived by car to have a picnic. She used to be an instructor at the Scottish Sailing Institute on Cumbrae and recognised us from a previous encounter off Largs when we had been fishing for mackerel from the canoe.

Camping by Loch Long

That evening we phoned to book a site at Ardgartan Club site explaining that we would be coming by canoe and would appreciate a pitch close to the entrance to the loch.

In the night we heard a tawny owl calling. In the morning it was replaced by a cuckoo. We had breakfast at 6.00 am and paddled north. When we camp wild we are scrupulous at making sure we leave no trace of our presence. It was a sunny morning with a convenient southerly breeze. Even though this beautiful loch is a naval dockyard we saw no signs of ships. Only a police motorboat patrolled. We ate lunch on the east side opposite the entrance to the beautiful Loch Goil and enjoyed the peace and majesty of the surrounding mountains.

We then resumed our northerly paddle and arrived at the Ardgartan Camp Site at about 2.00 pm. We waited for the occupants of the pitch near the gate to leave, (They had paid for two nights so they could stay longer) and put up our tent where they had been. We showered and enjoyed an ice cream as it was very hot.

The following morning we were off, without breakfast, at 5.00am. In the still morning we paddled across to Arrochar. We portaged the canoe on its small trolley to Tarbet and breakfasted by Loch Lomond.

Portaging at Arrochar

Then we set off the opposite way to the one described in our last voyage in these parts (see page 185ff). We paddled up Loch Lomond to Inversnaid. Again we were in glorious mountains. Opposite Inversnaid is the Inveruglas Hydro-electric Power Station with its great pipes running down Ben Vorlich from Loch Sloy. We watched a small Inversnaid Hotel motor boat trying to tow their large motor cruiser. We thought their tow rope was too short. Whatever the reason, the result was that every small jerk of the bigger boat turned the smaller one round so it was facing in the wrong direction. We left them to it and paddled into the wee harbour.

The harbour at Inversnaid

We took the canoe out of the water up the slipway and then on a seriously steep slope up to the hotel. Elisa from Hungary served us cheese sandwiches and iced drinks. The road behind the hotel was also very steep, and we made slow progress up it with continual rests.

Richard had greased the axle of the canoe-trolley before we left home, and was disappointed when it began to squeak as we went up the hill. Soon the squeak ceased being intermittent and became continuous. He called at a cottage where an Eastern European man sent us to a farmhouse where Richard found a lady struggling to remove the regulator from her gas barbecue. He asked whether she had any lubricating grease for our canoe trolley. She said, "You get this thing off. I will fetch some." We both did, and we greased the axle again.

Continuing up the hill we soon came to a dam marking the beginning of Loch Arklet. It was easy to launch and delightful to be paddling again. The loch is about 4 km long but the road deviates slightly from its eastern end. So we had to carry some of our gear and slide the canoe over some rough tussocky ground to get back to the road. We chatted for a few minutes to a wildlife ranger who was observing a buzzard's nest through his binoculars. Then we descended to Stronachlachar controlling the descent with a long strap attached to the stern of the canoe.

By now sadly the squeak had returned. We met a gentleman in his garden and apologised for the squeak. He fetched some WD40, which proved effective, and we were quiet for the rest of the expedition, and very pleased. On the pier we found that Loch Katrine was about 2 metres below. So we took out the cargo and lowered the canoe on straps. Richard climbed down into the canoe, and Celia lowered everything to him. We always fix everything securely with elastic cords. Then we paddled along the loch until we found a beach on which we set up camp.

Camping beside Loch Katrine

We always put our karrimats under the tent to protect the groundsheet when we are camping on rough ground or a stony beach. Tent pegs don't have much grip on sand or small stones so we make sure there is always something heavy in the tent so it doesn't blow away!

We woke early to still sunshine. Then we paddled all the way along Loch Katrine. The only ripples were created by our canoe and the reflections of the surrounding mountains were amazing. The lady wrestling with her gas cylinder had asked Richard why we put ourselves through all this work on a hot day when we could have stayed at home. The answer was available this morning as we paddled in total delight.

Reflections on Loch Katrine

Because we had been assured that the river out of Loch Katrine, the Achray Water, would be dry, we landed behind the steamship Sir Walter Scott in order to portage on the road. We learnt that, "during the course of the last two winters, extensive refurbishment of the Sir Walter Scott's hull had been completed, and the ship's entire superstructure had been rebuilt. New boilers had also been installed to ensure the future operational life of the ship, which had been converted from being fuelled by coal to being powered by bio-fuel, hoping for real benefits in terms of economy, cleanliness, and environmental impact. This process included the complete overhaul of the ship's original 1899 triple expansion steam engine, work which was completed by the Sir Walter Scott's own engineers." The final phase of the project also included the addition of a new enclosed lounge area in the forward part of the ship, "designed specifically to enhance the experience of a cruise on Loch Katrine for visitors" (i.e. to keep them dry!). The ship was looking very smart.

There was no danger of them getting wet today. It was dry and hot so we awarded ourselves cold drinks in this short encounter with civilisation. We sat in the shade and watched the visitors to the Trossachs who were surely not having such a wonderful experience as we. Then we set off down the road. We were glad it was not busy and glad also that the hills were quite gentle. The road was also shady. We chatted to a couple from Whitehaven who were thinking of retiring to Scotland.

At the junction with the road linking Aberfoyle and Callander we met an elderly couple who were staying in the Holiday Property Bond mansion at Brig O'Turk, formerly The Trossachs Hotel. It was the location for St. Catherine's School for Girls in John Buchan's "39 Steps", where Richard Hannay (played by Kenneth More) gave his impromptu lecture on the joys of the Spleanwort. Various other places on our route also featured in this film.

The couple told us that we could use the track from the mansion to Loch Achray. We soon arrived at the magnificent mansion, but found the gate to the track locked. One of the staff asked the manager who asked him to open the gate for us. The grounds were so pleasant that we slightly extended our permission and enjoyed a picnic lunch by the loch. One of the guests, a lady whose husband had died recently spoke with us. She was entertaining her young Swedish grandson. Both were interested in our trip and waved us goodbye as we set off along the loch.

Paddling on Loch Achray

It is less than 2km long and we were soon on the Black Water which flows out of it to Loch Venachar. The Black Water is very overgrown, with trees fallen across the stream in some places. Fortunately the burn was not flowing too fast and we were able to negotiate the obstacles.

The Black Water

As we emerged on to Loch Venachar the wind sprang up from behind, and Celia used a karrimat as a sail to speed us on our way. There were several green motor boats carrying fishermen. Halfway down the 6km loch the wind reversed and freshened so we reverted to paddling. It was really hard work and after a few minutes we headed for the shore and made a cup of tea. We were told later that the banks of the loch provided favourite venues for parties. It seemed that all the party-goers had left their portable barbecues, cans, bottles and other litter. It was a terrible mess.

After an hour the wind had dropped and we continued on our way to a beach at the eastern end of the loch. There were 3 groups of sunbathers, all of whom were surprised at our emergence and interested in our expedition. We were soon portaging again along the quiet lane because the river from Loch Venachar, the Eas Gobhain had little water in it. After less than 2km we came to Trossachs Tryst, a high quality hostel offering single, family and dormitory accommodation. It was very pleasant and we stayed the night there, catering for ourselves as were the other guests, with cereals, fruit juice and beverages provided for breakfast. The cost was £17.50 each, which we thought good value.

Because we were catering for ourselves there was no problem with our rising at 4.30 am, having breakfast, and being on our way just after 5. We continued down the lane and came to a track through the woods to the Eas Gobhain. We found it with plenty of water and launched the canoe. It was a little overgrown but passable and soon we were on the River Teith through Callander. It looked placid and wide, giving no hints of the excitement to come.

We had enjoyed no rain for some days and the river was fairly low. This meant that we had to stop several times to help the canoe over banks of shingle. It also meant that many rocks were exposed in the faster flowing sections. The Scottish Canoe Association booklet describes it as a beginner's white water river. Several places marked as weirs on the Ordnance Survey map have no weir but a rapid with exposed and slightly submerged rocks. We negotiated these with a combination of judgement and luck.

When a river winds the water is deepest and flows fastest round the outside of the bends. Sometimes there was a shingle bank sloping down toward the outside of a bend where trees and brambles hung low over the river. We did not want to canoe through these as experience had taught us that it was difficult to avoid capsizing there. We also knew that if we tried to canoe too high on the shingle bank away from these overhanging branches we were likely to be propelled sideways by the flow coming off the shingle bank. So we chose a path close to these overhanging trees but not touching them and were pleased to be successful and dry.

We had read about the Torrie Rapid which used to be a slalom course. It has a ledge on the left and requires a sharp turn to the right at the end, in low water, to avoid some undercut rock. In high water a standing wave train is set up. For us the river was between these extremes and we emerged safely.

Deanston Weir can be dangerous in flood. If the water is low one can land on the left and take the canoe down the dry weir. If the river is in flood one is supposed to land on the right and walk the canoe down the salmon leap using lines to the prow and the stern. Water was flowing down the face of the weir and a little water was flowing down the fish leap so we decided to canoe down this. It was a bumpy ride. At the bottom we got out and walked precariously on the slippery walls separating the pools of the leap. We then guided the canoe with our straps tied at stem and stern over the final waterfall.

DeanstonWeir salmon leap

Small rapids on the River Teith

We enjoyed the River Teith though we had to keep our wits about us all the way. It was very beautiful and we enjoyed several sightings of dippers bobbing on the rocks. We stopped for lunch at Doune Castle and spoke to a lady who said she had canoed on the River Danube. She was throwing a ball into the water for her dog. Once it was not interested so we retrieved it for her. She did not learn and promptly threw the ball in the river again!

Eventually we joined the River Forth. The river became slow moving and placid. At the bridge which carries the M9 over the Forth the river became tidal so we considered that at this point we had achieved our intention of going from coast to coast. We pulled over into the reeds for a celebratory cup of tea. At once a head appeared above us inviting us to come round the corner where there was a place we could land with seats to sit on. We paddled round and found two fishermen, a beach and two wooden benches. We thanked them. Fishermen are not always friendly to canoeists. In retrospect, this would have been a good place to camp for the night.

After chatting to them we set off again. According to our (incorrect!) reading of the tide table it was high water and we thought the lowering tide would help our progress on the tedious meanders round Stirling. We had assumed that the river would be benign but one of the fishermen said there was a tricky section just round the next corner. There was a weir marked on the map but it looked defunct. We would have been wise to walk ahead on the bank and inspect it.

We didn't. We canoed on. Just round the bend the river began to flow swiftly down a slope. This was a surprise as we thought it was high tide. We slalomed between rocks for about 100 metres. And then the canoe tipped up and we went over quite a high weir. The water was boiling furiously at the bottom. Our concern was that the canoe would bury its nose in the water and we would get wet. But the wonderful vessel looked after us, stayed straight and true, and though some water came aboard we carried on safely down the river.

As we continued we noticed that the banks had become quite high and were lined with terrible thick and lugubrious mud. We came to the old Stirling Bridge, quickly followed by the new road bridge and the one carrying the railway.

The old Stirling Bridge

We paddled on looking for somewhere to get off the river. As the tide fell the banks became higher and muddier. Several times we stopped by a pile of stones and tried to get out – but the mud was dreadful. I expect we could have got out but would not have been able to get the canoe and our kit out too. On we went. We formed a fairly desperate plan. If we could get near a road and wait on the river till high water (at about 2.00am!) we would be able to get off easily. This was the only plan we could think of – short of canoeing all night. Things were not looking good.

Then we canoed round a bend and saw a rowing boat on the river. We paddled up to it and said to the oarsman,

"Either you are in the same fix as us, or you know a way off the river."

He said, "I know a way off the river."

He told us to paddle on for about 100 metres to a bank of stones and he would come and help us in 10 minutes.

His son stood on the shore holding one end of a net. He took the other end of the net and rowed round, laying out the net in a semi-circle. Then they pulled the net in and retrieved the contents of the net. It was a method of fishing we had seen and even helped with in West Africa – but we are not sure it is legal in Scotland.

We didn't watch but waited for the man where he had told us to. We took some of our cargo on a path through some woodland and giant hemlock – making sure we did not touch it because we had heard that it could damage skin seriously. The man and his son arrived carrying large heavy looking bags. We did not ask what was in them. They took their catch to a van down the path and returned to help us. We could not have managed on our own. They helped with the kit and then lifted the canoe high over a fence and to a track at the other end of the path.

Whatever they had been doing we were very grateful to them for their assistance. We phoned some friends and they kindly took us and the canoe to their home in Burntisland.

We had intended to canoe all the way to Burntisland down the Firth of Forth, but a fresh Easterly breeze was setting itself up and the Forth is an exposed estuary. Our friends had offered to collect us if conditions became untenable. We decided that we had had an enjoyable trip and now was the time to stop.

Loving our neighbour

In Luke chapter 10 of the Bible Jesus tells an expert in the Law that the two most important things for us to do are to `Love the Lord our God with the whole of our being;' and to `Love our neighbour as much as ourself.'

Like the expert in the law Christians must ask, "Who is my neighbour?" How did Jesus answer? He told a story – the story of the Good Samaritan.

In 586 BC the Babylonians under King Nebuchadnezzar invaded Jerusalem, destroyed the temple and carried away a sizeable proportion of the population into slavery. While this was a traumatic event for the Jews it caused a development of their religion and understanding of God.

When they returned in 539 BC with the permission of the Persian king Cyrus the Great they rebuilt the temple and were ready to accept the writings of the prophets and the Wisdom literature as Holy Scripture. The Samaritans were some of the people who were not exiled. They remained faithful to the Pentateuch – the first five books of the Bible – without adding to them. They still do the same today – living in and around Nābulus on the West Bank of the Jordan. Sadly the relationships between Jews and Samaritans deteriorated so that in Jesus' time they hated each other.

In answer to the question, "Who is my neighbour?" Jesus told the story of a Jewish man who was mugged while travelling on the road. Neither a priest nor a Levite helped him, doubtless for their own reasons of religion or safety. But, of all people, a Samaritan, one who was beneath contempt, gave him first aid and took him to a place where he paid for him to have continued treatment. To Jesus' question who it was who was neighbour to the man who was mugged the expert in the Law answered, "The one who showed mercy on him."

We understand our task as Christians is to love and serve God and to bring others to love him too; and to love our neighbour – even the one we hadn't thought of – as much as we love ourselves. In a sermon at St John's Church, Largs on 11 July 2010 Richard asked the congregation, "Who is our neighbour?" Here are some of his suggested answers.

"Our neighbour is the person who lives near us who could do with a hand. They may be sick or housebound and need friendship, visiting, help with shopping or gardening.

Some neighbours are members of our family. We parents and grandparents have a tremendous responsibility to our children and grandchildren, not so much to give them money and things, but to give them ourselves. To show them what is really significant. So we will listen to them, be interested in them; show them that real relationships are more fun than fashionable things or money.

Our neighbour is a teenager in our church. Do we know his/her name? Do we speak to him? Do we greet him by name? Do the youngsters feel they are members of the church because of the welcome we give them? Or it may be an adult in the church? Do we know their names? Are we interested in those who sit near us? Do we care about them?

Our neighbour is the person who lives fairly near us who is not much like us. They may not go to church. They may be out of work. They may be young. We may suspect they do things we might not approve of. Jesus instructs us to love them. How do you think he would like us to do that?

Our neighbour may be in prison. The early church was especially keen on looking after those Christians who were in prison because of their faith. Today in Britain it is illegal to discriminate on grounds of faith – but that is not true everywhere. Today across the world thousands are imprisoned because they are Christians, or for some other innocent reason; and some are tortured. One way to love them would be to join Amnesty International and write to governments to ask for their release, or if the prisoner is accused of committing an offence, for a fair trial. If you have access to the internet you could look on the Amnesty website to find out about these people and contact their government.

Our neighbour might live in a poorer country. One way we can love them is to make a serious commitment to them through Christian Aid. And we can buy fairly-traded goods. Some of the big multinational companies who grow bananas do not even remove their workers from the banana plantations when they are spraying them with pesticides. And those workers are paid a pittance. You can buy fairly-traded bananas and other fruit from the supermarket. These folk will receive a fairer price for their labour and also a payment to their community to install a water borehole, clinic or school. The ordinary tea which you might be buying provides very small wages for the pickers. There is a huge British Company, working in Assam and supplying most of our popular brands of tea, which pays as little as 40 pence for a 12 hour day. And this level of wages is typical for growers of many of our basic products: tea, coffee, chocolate, sugar, dried fruit, bananas, pineapples etc. We believe that making sure we only buy fairly-traded goods, where they are available, is part of the duty of Christian disciples. That is what we believe. What do you think?

Our neighbour may not be born yet. He or she may be your great great grandchild. God calls us to love these people too. Our generation is using up the earth like no generation before it. At the present rate of consumption, in 100 years time there will be no oil, little coal, and no uranium for nuclear fuel. Already we are extracting fossil fuels from more and more difficult places – like the bottom of the sea or the arctic – and mining these areas involves catastrophic environmental damage, not just when things go wrong but all the time. Even using fossil-fuels is raising the temperature of the air and causing violent storms and periods of drought. Sea levels are rising and flooding is increasing in low-lying areas.

Loving our neighbour involved us writing a letter of objection to the application by Ayrshire Power to build a coal fired power station at Hunterston, not because it is in our backyard, but because, in burning fossil fuels unnecessarily, we are taking a vital resource from our children, who will need them for paint, plastics and drugs. And loving these neighbours of the future might involve us in deliberately reducing our own carbon footprint.

Loving our Neighbour might involve us in doing things we might think of as political rather than spiritual. It might take us into protest as we did with other members of Amnesty in 2009 when we dressed in orange suits and knelt in the road in front of the American consulate in Edinburgh to protest about the continued detention of people without trial in Guantanamo Bay in Cuba. It might take us into making decisions about what we eat. We personally will not buy a pineapple unless it has been fairly-traded, because we want to love our neighbour.

So I am asking you to think seriously about these things. I'm not asking you to follow me. I'm asking you to follow Jesus as his disciple. And if we do that we may find ourselves making some unexpected decisions and taking some unexpected actions."

In our previous book *Walkers on Water* [5] we wrote: *We, personally, use public transport where possible and only use our camper occasionally. We walk or cycle short distances. Our house has mainly low energy light bulbs. We are intending to improve the insulation of our house and consider installing solar panels for heating water. We support Greenpeace and Friends of the Earth. We try to buy locally produced, organic or*

Fairly-Traded food where possible. We must think about further actions we can take to reduce the size of our footprint on the earth and to help others.

Lowering our Carbon Footprint

On Monday 20 October 2008 builders arrived and unloaded some very heavy steel beams in order to begin altering our house to lower its carbon footprint and provide other improvements.

We had begun thinking what we could do almost as soon as we saw the bungalow we had bought in Largs. As well as eco-things we wanted to increase our storage space for the things for our hobbies: sailing, canoeing, paragliding etc. We also had only one bathroom with the only toilet in it. We felt it would be good to have more – especially when we entertained visitors.

We were recommended a retired architect, who lived in Largs, and we discussed our plans with him. The most important thing he explained to us was that if we were installing a staircase it should follow the roofline otherwise it would occupy a large amount of space upstairs. It was he who suggested the stairs should come out of the kitchen rather than the hall which had been our original intention. He drew up some plans which involved us extending the roof of the bungalow at the north, east and south with a short ridge and a gable at the west. This would give us a large south-facing roof for solar panels, a room with a view over the Firth of Clyde, a bathroom, study and storage space. But he said it would not be passed by the planners as the roof was being raised in height by just over a metre.

And then sadly he became ill with cancer and died. We appointed a firm of architects to redraw the plans and presented them to the North Ayrshire Council. They said the changes were incongruous, and detrimental to the road, and refused planning permission. We had built a balsa model of the roof and showed it to all six contiguous neighbours. All of them had liked what we proposed and thought it looked neat. So we appealed to the Scottish Government. A reporter whose job was to read submissions from the council and us and to decide between them came and decided that the appeal should be allowed.

The final task before finding a builder was to get a consulting engineer to draw up structural plans and have them approved too. This was a very slow business and so several years elapsed between us deciding what we wanted to do and the builders arriving.

The building work we had chosen to undertake was very intrusive. Every room required alteration, and we continued living in the house for the seven months that the builders were with us. We enjoyed them even though we could rarely understand their speech as they came from East Ayrshire, whose dialect we found impenetrable.

A short break from building

Hugh, the boss, fitting a worktop in the kitchen

The borehole drill

A borehole 100 metres deep was drilled for a heat pump, in the back garden. This required a machine, which looked as if it had come from the Battle of the Somme, to get into the back garden. We dismantled a fence and a low wall. As well as bringing up 3 tonnes of mud it brought up 100 tonnes of water. The result was a mess – which eventually required us to clean the 500,000 stones in our drying area under the clothes line - a task that occupied about 1000 hours. Richard personally dug the trench and a metre cube hole to enable the pipe connecting the borehole to the heat pump to be laid.

A firm agreed to deliver the heat pump on 27 October but they had made a computer error and it was not in their warehouse. We received it on 16 December. In the meantime we had become very cold and eventually unwell. We put up a tent of sheets inside the kitchen and called the space inside it *a yurt*. We warmed it with an electric radiator and put on coats, gloves and hats when we ventured out into the rest of the house.

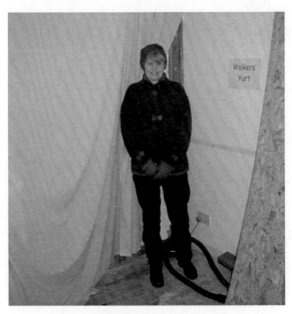

Celia at the entrance to *the yurt*

Eventually the heat pump was installed. It takes low temperature heat from the borehole and provides higher temperature hot water for radiators and the taps. It is about 400% efficient, so for 1 kwh electricity it provides 4 kwh heat. We transferred our electricity supply to Good Energy [9] so that heating our house and water became 100% renewable.

We put two sets of solar panels on the new enlarged south facing roof. The Solartwin [10] solar thermal panel takes water from the bottom of the hot water cylinder, heats it and places it in the top of the cylinder. The water is pumped by a tiny solar-driven pump. The panel is flexible and can withstand being frozen. Because there is no secondary coil and the hot water is placed at the top of the cylinder, to which the hot taps are connected, hot water is available for use very quickly on sunny days.

The solar panels

228

Also on the roof are 16 photo-voltaic panels which produce up to 2 kilo-watts of electricity. It is connected to the National Grid, and Good Energy pays us for all the electricity we generate. They also give us a small annual payment for the hot water supplied by the solar thermal panel.

Other eco-improvements we made were to use very low energy led lights, and insulate the walls, and the roof-space to a depth of 30 cm. All this was very expensive so we took out a mortgage to help pay for it.

The way we see this is that as well as giving us an improved house to live in with more storage space, more bathrooms, laundry and drying room, and an improved kitchen, we now have a house which is carbon-neutral in its use. We rarely use our camper, and walk, cycle, and use public transport whenever possible. So we are attempting to love our neighbour of the future. We also buy fairly-traded items as well as organic and local things, and grow as much as we can in our garden. This helps us to love our poorer neighbour overseas.

Now and Then

As we write this book we have passed our 66th birthdays. Of course this is not old in the West of the 21st century. But we are definitely not as young as we were when we could walk 30 miles in a day or climb to 3000 metres carrying a paraglider. Physically and mentally we have to accept our limitations.

We have retired from paragliding, and we suspect that the physical expeditions we undertake are mainly in the past. Apart from these things we are reasonably fit and well. We walk short distances; cycle further; and we can still be seen paddling the canoe on the sea in front of our house, sometimes catching mackerel. We cultivate the garden and grow a good selection of vegetables. We read magazines and books. We watch the birds that come to our feeders and those we see on the shore. Recently we have begun to keep records of bumblebees, which we send to the Bumble Bee Conservation Trust, as we send in bird records to the British Trust for Ornithology.

We work with the Africa Committee at church and have a relationship with some people and communities in Ghana and Malawi. Richard does some preaching and leads services when clergy are away. We use the internet to try to influence the decisions of governments and businesses on behalf of Amnesty International, Greenpeace, Friends of the Earth and Avaaz.

We have also visited our son Justin, in the Gambia, and when he moved to South America, in Chile. This involves us in flying long distances, which, sadly, blows a hole in our low carbon-use intentions!

We continue to love one another and enjoy one another's company as well as having friends in Largs and further afield. We take an interest in our sons and keep in contact with them and others by visits, letters, emails, texts and Skype.

What the future holds we do not know. We will try to walk in the light of the Lord, knowing his love and being his ambassadors in this dark world. We do know that the future and we are in God's hands. One day we will experience light without shadows or darkness and we will be with him for ever.

References

1   Great Expectations by Charles Dickens

2   Emma by Jane Austen

3   Watership Down by Richard Adams published by Puffin Books, 1973

4   The Lighthouse Stevensons by Bella Bathurst, Harper Collins Publishers Ltd (6 April 1999) ISBN: 978-0002570060

5   Walkers on Water by Richard and Celia Walker. This book can be obtained from us. (see page 232)

6   The Faith of Edward Wilson by George Seaver published by John Murray, Albemarle Street, London, March 1948

7   A History of Bilston, in the County of Stafford. A record of its archæology, ecclesiology, etc. (1893) by George T. Lawley

8   John Wilkinson by Ron Davies (Dulston Press - 1987)

9   Good Energy, Monkton Reach, Monkton Hill, Chippenham, Wiltshire SN15 1EE

10 Solar Twin Ltd, 50 Watergate Street, Chester, CH1 2LA, UK

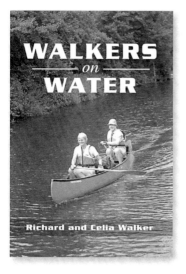

Walkers on Water is an opportunity to go with us on three of our recent adventures. The first is aboard a Bavaria 31 yacht from Plymouth to Lézardrieux in Brittany via Guernsey (and back!); the second is in our Wayfarer sailing dinghy, cruising and camping on board, between Helford River and Plymouth. The third is by open canoe from Bradley near Wolverhampton to Guildford in Surrey, camping in a small tent. We write about the history of the places we travel through as well as details of canoe-camping.

The book is a paperback with 180 pages. It is lavishly illustrated with photos. The price of the book is £12.50, plus £1.50 for post and packing for one book; further copies 75p extra. This includes an immediate donation of at least £4 for WaterAid. Eventually all proceeds will go to WaterAid.

Water Aid is an international charity that provides clean water and sanitation for some of the poorest people on earth. People accepting copies have already given over £7,100 to Water Aid (April 2011) – including tax reclaimed - through our books.

If you would like a copy of Walkers on Water please send a cheque for £14.00 with your name and address to

Richard and Celia Walker,
10 Rockland Park, Largs, Ayrshire KA30 8HB

If you pay UK income tax and would like WaterAid to reclaim by Gift Aid the tax that you have paid, please say so.

Or look at and order securely through our website
http://richardandceliawalkerbooks.webplus.net